VoIP

Cisco Unified Communications Manager Express
A Hands-On Approach

Milos Ockay, Ph.D.

Cisco is trademark of Cisco Systems, Inc. in U.S. and other countries.
Windows is trademark of the Microsoft group companies.
Linux is registered trademark of Linus Torvalds in U.S. and other countries.
PuTTY is copyright 1997-2018 Simon Tatham.
CreateSpace and CreateSpace Logo are trademarks of On-Demand Publishing LLC.

ISBN-13: 9781729650851
ISBN-10: 1729650856

Amazon Digital Services LLC. CreateSpace Independent Publishing Platform, Seattle.
Printed by CreateSpace, An Amazon.com Company.
Text printed in the United States.
First printing, November 2018.

Available from Amazon.com, CreateSpace.com, and other retail outlets.

Author
Milos Ockay, Ph.D.

Editor
Anna Dzurova

Design, Layout and Cover
Mnemonix

Reviewers
prof. Ing. Stanislav Marchevský, CSc.
doc. Ing. Pavel Segeč, Ph.D.

To my wonderful Anna

"Intentionally blank"

Contents

ACKNOWLEDGEMENTS

First and foremost, I would like to thank my dad and my beloved Anna for standing beside me throughout my life and career. I'd like to also thank her for editorial work on this book. I'd like to thank my boss who always finds the way to support my work with up to date software and hardware and for his help to make this book reality. I'd really like to thank all of my colleges, who are the part of supportive and creative workspace. All of them are great persons and scholars and they are one of the reasons that I like what I do. I also wish to thank all of my reviewers for devoting their time and efforts towards this book. I owe a huge thanks to Cisco Systems, Inc. and the Cisco's community for providing the knowledge base, great ideas and support.

ABOUT THE AUTHOR

Milos Ockay received an M.S. in Electronics and Telecommunication Systems from Armed Forces Academy of Liptovsky Mikulas in 2003 and Ph.D. in Informatics from Technical University of Kosice in 2012. Since 2006 he has worked as an assistant professor at the Armed Forces Academy of Liptovsky Mikulas. He is also a long term CCNA and VoIP instructor. When he is not coding, configuring or teaching, he can be found making 3D models, running, working out or practicing Tae Kwon Do.

ABOUT THIS BOOK

INTRODUCTORY CHAPTER

Fellow reader, I am glad that this book caught your attention and you decided to open it. In this chapter I would like to answer a few questions which may and, surely, will arise at the beginning of your learning path.

❖ What is VoIP?

In the 1990s, an interest in carrying voice over Internet Protocol (IP) networks appeared. This technology is commonly referred to as VoIP today. Voice over Internet Protocol (VoIP) uses IP to carry digitally encoded voice. The VoIP system offers many benefits: Single communications network for telephones and computers, new features, applications and capabilities, just to name a few. [1]

❖ Is this book a right choice to achieve your learning goals?

This book was written for absolute VoIP beginners who have no previous experience with it. However, slight Information Technologies (IT) or networking background is welcomed. Of course, you can start to study this book without any, but you will surly struggle with some problems and you will also need to study other sources which are considered IT essentials. Essential knowledge base is briefly covered in Chapter 1 and it should give you a starting point even if you lack some IT knowledge. If you already completed Cisco Certified Network Associate (CCNA) or an equivalent course, you are very well equipped and you can start without hesitation.

❖ What will you learn?

This book is here to teach you to configure Cisco Unified Communications Manager Express (CUCME). In the scope of protocols, this book can be possibly divided into three parts. The first part deals with the Signaling Connection Control Part (SCCP) configuration tasks. The second part is side-by-side Session Initiation Protocol (SIP) variant of the first part. The third part presents so-called hybrid configuration tasks, where both protocols coexist in CUCME. This usually happens during the migration process from one protocol to another. This book covers a wide range of configuration tasks from basic to advanced ones. After completing this book, you should be able to create functional VoIP solution and you should be able to administrate it.

❖ How will you learn it?

This book uses the hands-on approach. Rather than presenting in depth theoretical knowledge, this book consists of well-structured, practical and fully solved configuration tasks. The goal of this book is to teach you practical skills to make VoIP work in real world. All chapters present you with just enough theoretical knowledge to achieve practical tasks. Further study sections direct you toward the theoretical knowledge you should study further.

There is the Quiz at the end of each chapter. It will test your knowledge and motivate you to study further. It is not simply enough just to read this book. You need to lay your hands on real networking hardware to achieve a desirable goal.

❖ What hardware and software should you use?

This book was written with hardware and software limitations in mind. In the lab environment, where multiple students (or a group of students) use the set of routers, switches and IP phones, the common problem with the number of devices arises. Usually it is impossible to let each student configure a separate set of devices in the same time. Virtualized solutions do not always substitute real hardware solutions. All the configuration tasks in this book use minimum possible number of devices to accomplish the task. Devices are also reused instead of constantly added. We also use the same types of IP phones to avoid repeated configuration tasks for each phone type separately. There is no software version mentioned in this book. It is because of keeping this book versatile and universal. You can use whatever type of hardware, Internetwork Operating System (IOS) version and firmware you like. BUT keep in mind if something is not working, check if it is supported by your version (it is usually well documented on the vendor website). Configurations in this book were checked and rechecked for functionality. If something is not working in your configuration it is most likely a version problem, typo or a missed line. We intentionally avoid the use of Graphical User Interface (GUI) in this book and stick to the Command Line Interface (CLI). Main reasons for this are that the GUI is constantly changing and we did not want to make this book time limited and full of pictures. If you master the VoIP principles on the CLI level, you should be able to use GUI without any problems. However, if you are looking for a GUI guide, this book is not your cup of tea. These preliminaries make this book an ideal study material for networking lab environments. But should not be afraid, it will equip you with skills and knowledge usable in enterprise environment. You need to learn the basics in simple environment to be successful in more complex and variable one.

❖ How to read this book?

All the configurations have strictly defined form of notation. At the beginning, there is a hostname of device we configure. In this example it is SWITCH_A. The acronym in the brackets clearly identifies the configuration within the scope of the book. The book also contains a configuration register. In this case ch2c9 means chapter two, configuration nine. All the configurations are easily distinguishable because of their gray background.

SWITCH_A config (ch2c9):

```
SWITCH_A#command1
SWITCH_A#command2
```

Black horizontal lines have also their meaning. Single configuration task can be divided into multiple sections. We use black horizontal line at the beginning and at the end of configuration. The configuration section without or with only one horizontal line is not considered a standalone piece. If you start entering this kind of configuration piece to your device, you will probably get an error message.

```
SWITCH_A#command3
SWITCH_A#command4
SWITCH_A#command5
```

Commands have to stay in order. It is critical to keep the order of commands to achieve the functional results.

```
SWITCH_A#command6
SWITCH_A#command7
```

Part of the command can be variable, meaning you need to enter your specific value (IP and MAC address, phone type and many more). All of these variables are <u>underlined</u>. We use *italics* for any command outside the gray configuration box and quiz. Command *telephony-service* is a good example.

❖ Before you start

Starting point is clearly defined at the beginning of each chapter. Usually telephony configuration of devices is wiped out and number of IP phones usually change. There are only slight network topology changes between the chapters, but it is good practice to check your wiring before you start a new chapter. You should check the capacity of flash card on your CME_ROUTER. There has to be enough space for IOS and firmware. The more different types of phones we use, the more space the firmware will consume.

PRELIMINARIES AND ESSENTIALS

CHAPTER 1

Chapter 1: PRELIMINARIES AND ESSENTIALS

As already has been mentioned, this book should serve as a starting point for readers with no experience in VoIP field. However, there is a considerable amount of essential networking knowledge required to fully understand VoIP basics. Readers who studied and passed CCNA or an equivalent course or already have working experience with the networking are well equipped for this book and they can skip this chapter without hesitation. For the rest of you this chapter summarizes the essentials, so you do not struggle with the following chapters because of the lack of the basic knowledge. This chapter does not make you the networking expert. It just provides you with enough information to be able to start with VoIP. You should keep this in mind and should not underestimate the further study suggestions. There are many online sources, where you can expand your knowledge far beyond the scope of this chapter.

- ❖ Media Access Control (MAC) address
- ❖ Internet Protocol (IP) address
- ❖ Dynamic Host Configuration Protocol (DHCP)
- ❖ Connect and wipe clean switch and router
- ❖ Virtual Local Area Networks (VLAN)
- ❖ VLAN Trunking Protocol (VTP)
- ❖ Routing Information Protocol (RIP)
- ❖ Cisco Unified Communications Manager Express (CUCME)
- ❖ SCCP and SIP
- ❖ Further study
- ❖ Quiz

❖ Media Access Control (MAC) address

A media access control (MAC) address is also called physical address. This address is unique among the manufactured network interfaces. MAC addresses are mostly assigned by the manufacturers of network interfaces and they are stored in the hardware. If the network device has multiple network interfaces, each interface has to have a unique MAC address. The most common format of MAC address forms six groups of hexadecimal digits known as octets. Each octet consists of 8 bits. 48 bits (6 octets x 8 bits) can possibly create address space which contains 2^{48} (281 474 976 710 656) addresses. [2]

Notations of MAC address:

d2:25:35:18:c9:ab   *d2-25-35-18-c9-ab*   *d225.3518.c9ab*

d2	25	35	18	c9	ab
1. octet 8 bits 11010010	2. octet 00100101	3. octet 00110101	4. octet 00011000	5. octet 11001001	6. octet 10101011
Organizationally Unique Identifier (OUI)			Network Interface Controller (NIC)		

The first three octets identify the organization that issued the NIC. This identifier is known as Organizationally Unique Identifier (OUI). Last three octets are assigned by the organization. 48 bit model will be replaced by 64 bit in the future with the possibility to assign locally administrated addresses by the administrator.

In the scope of this book, MAC addresses are used to clearly identify IP phones and associate directory numbers with the specific IP phones. MAC address of the IP phone can be found on the sticker on the back of the IP phone or in the phone's menu. Common practice in lab testing and learning environment is to write the MAC address on the front of the phone, thus we always see it during the frequent configuration changes. We can use post-it notes or other office stickers for this purpose.

d225.3518.c9ab

❖ Internet Protocol (IP) address

An Internet Protocol (IP) address is numerical address assigned to each device participating in a network communication. Address serves the purpose of identifying and locating the devices. IP address is being analyzed multiple times by intermediary devices (routers and switches). IP address version 4 is defined as a 32 bit binary number which forms four groups of eight binary numbers separated by the dots. Address space defined by 32 bits contains 2^{32} (4 294 967 296) addresses. [2]

Dotted binary notation:

11000000.10101000.00000000.00000011

Decimal equivalent is frequently used (dotted decimal notation):

192.168.0.3

1. octet	2. octet	3. octet	4. octet
11000000	10101000	00000000	00000011
192	168	0	3

IP address uses the 32 bit mask to separate network bits from host bits. Mask bits with value equal to 1 represents the network bits in the IP address and mask bits with the value equal to 0 represent the host bits in the IP address.

For example:

IP Address

1. octet	2. octet	3. octet	4. octet
11000000	10101000	00000000	00000011
192	168	0	3

Mask

1. octet	2. octet	3. octet	4. octet
11111111	11111111	11111111	00000000
255	255	255	0

This means that the first three octets are used for identifying the network and the last octet is devoted for the hosts. The mask is frequently represented in the form of prefix. 192.168.0.3/24 is the same as the IP address 192.168.0.3 with the mask 255.255.255.0 it means that 24 bits are used for the network and 8 bits (32-24) are used for the hosts. 0 (00000000) and 255 (11111111) combinations of the host bits are reserved for special purpose (network identification and the broadcast). The remaining combinations give us 254 host addresses for the devices (from 192.168.0.1 to 192.168.0.254). Of course, there are the networks with more than 254 devices connected to it. In that case we need to use more host bits and less network bits in the mask to include more devices in the network. It is important for the successful communication between devices to choose IP addresses from the same network (for example 192.168.0.5/24 and 192.168.0.200/24). If the devices have addresses chosen from the different networks (e.g. 172.20.35.20/22 and 192.168.1.56/24) it is necessary to include the intermediary device (router) with the active routing protocol to ensure successful communication across the networks. IP address must be locally unique. This means that the same IP address cannot be used for multiple devices within the same network. Detailed description of the network addressing and sub netting is out of the scope of this book. In this book we use multiple IP version 4 address ranges to separate the data from the voice. We use the 24 bits masks and stay in 254 host range to keep addressing scheme simple and comprehensible.

❖ Dynamic Host Configuration Protocol (DHCP)

IP address has to be assigned to the device. We have basically two options how to do that. At first, IP addresses can by assigned to the devices manually. Each device has a command or configuration menu which allows us to enter IP address and the mask. This task usually requires administrator (root) access rights. Manual (static) assignment can be used in the small network with few interconnected devices.

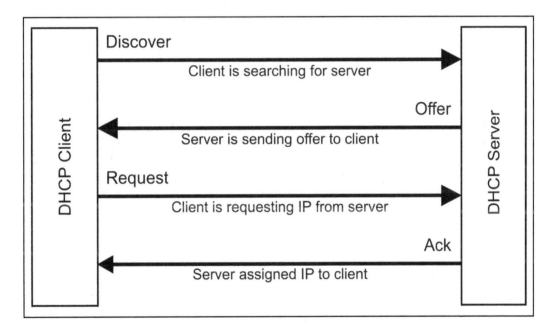

Figure 1: DHCP

In the large, quickly changing network it is almost impossible to keep consistent static assignment of IP addresses. Dynamic assignment of IP addresses is a far more suitable option for large networks. Dynamic Host Configuration Protocol (DHCP) is used for automatic address assignment. Devices ask the DHCP server for the IP address. Server chooses the unused IP address from the IP pool and leases the address to the device. In our configuration, one of the routers will serve as DHCP server for the PCs and IP phones. PCs and IP phones will use separate DHCP pools, hence we will use different networks to differentiate data and voice traffic. [3]

❖ Connect and wipe clean switch and router

In order to successfully accomplish complex configuration tasks we need to know how to connect and wipe switch and router clean. PC which we use for configuration of switch or router has to have serial console client program installed (we use PuTTY) and rollover cable connected to the serial port or to the USB to Serial adapter (Fig. 2). Standalone USB rollover cable is also the option, which is basically combination of two cables mentioned before. Other side of rollover cable is connected to the RJ45 console port of the switch or router. A console port is often marked with the turquoise color.

Figure 2: Rollover cable and USB to Serial adapter

Now we can run the serial console program on the PC. The connection requires a correct setting of COM port (Fig. 3). We can obtain COM port number by checking port settings in your system device manager. After we open connection, PC connects to the switch or the router and the console window is displayed. The booting process on switch or router takes some time. We need to press the RETURN key few times until the following prompt is displayed and we can enter the commands.

```
switch>

or

router>
```

The current configuration of switch or router does not have to necessary reflect our needs or it can even spoil the configuration of other devices connected to the network. We need to wipe the configuration of the device clean. We need to erase startup configuration of device and reload it.

```
switch>enable
switch#delete flash:vlan.dat
switch#erase startup-config
switch#reload
Proceed with reload? [confirm]<enter>
```

Router procedure is the same but VLAN part is omitted because there is no VLAN configuration required on router.

```
router>enable
router#erase startup-config
router#reload
Proceed with reload? [confirm]<enter>
```

Basic configuration also requires securing your switch or router, but we leave it unprotected to keep configurations as simple as possible. In enterprise environment, however, it is absolutely necessary to secure all the devices connected to the network.

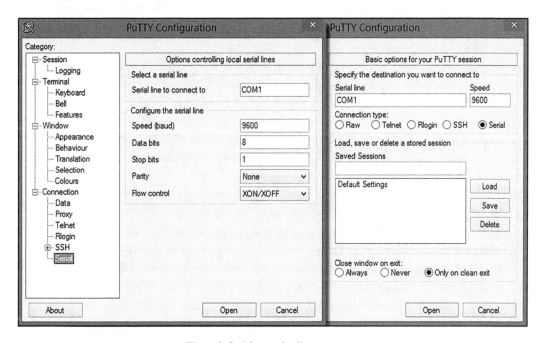

Figure 3: Serial console client program

❖ Virtual Local Area Networks (VLAN)

VoIP topology isolates data and voice traffic to separate networks. It is almost impossible physically separate networks, especially in large installments. Physical topology usually reflects enterprise structure and we need to integrate many services within the single media and keep reasonable redundancy level. Virtual Local Area Networks (VLANs) solve the problem by separating the networks virtually. VLANs are configured on switches hence the whole concept operates on Open Systems Interconnection (OSI) layer 2. Some of the network links have to transport packets for more than one VLAN, but they use only one physical connection. This type of link is called trunk. On each end of the link the packets are marked with a special tag. Tags are used on the other side of the link to distinguish various VLANs. [4]

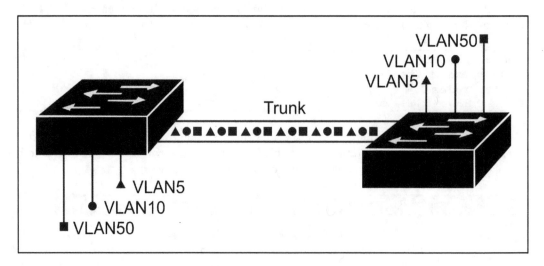

Figure 4: VLAN trunk

❖ VLAN Trunking Protocol (VTP)

One way how to configure VLANs is to configure the same set of VLANS on each switch. On few switches, it is a simple configuration task, but the painful one with many switches included in a network. VLAN Trunking Protocol (VTP) provides the effective way to automatically distribute VLAN configuration across the network. We need to choose one of the switches as the VTP server. The rest of the switches will play the role of clients. VLAN configuration is done only on server and it will be distributed automatically to clients.

❖ Routing Information Protocol (RIP)

Routing is a process of selecting the best paths to the destination in a network. Routing directs packets through intermediary devices (routers). Routing protocols specify rules how the routing is done. They use the specific algorithms and metrics to accomplish the task. In our configuration, we use the Routing Information Protocol (RIP) to route the packets among the VLANs. RIP is a distance-vector routing protocol which uses the hop count as a routing metric. [4]

❖ Cisco Unified Communications Manager Express (CUCME)

Cisco Unified Communications Manager Express (CUCME) is a call-processing application that enables Cisco routers to deliver key-system or hybrid Private Branch eXchange (PBX) functionality. It is a feature-rich entry-level IP telephony solution and it is integrated directly into Cisco IOS software. CUCME offers most of the core telephony features required in a small office, and also many advanced features not available with traditional telephony solutions. [5]

❖ SCCP and SIP

Skinny Connection Control Protocol (SCCP) and Session Initiation Protocol (SIP) are the network layer communication protocols. Their most common applications are in internet telephony. SCCP is Cisco proprietary protocol used for control of phones connected to CUCME. Cisco has been moving to replace SCCP with SIP in most instances for actual call establishment, while physical keys, soft keys, and user interface elements are managed through other proprietary mechanisms. SIP defines the messages that are sent between endpoints, which govern establishment, termination and other essential elements of a call. This book presents both protocols in side-by-side fashion.

❖ Further study

Information presented in this chapter should be sufficient enough to proceed to the next chapter. However, further study of following subjects is advised.

- Basic configuration of switch and router
- ISO/OSI and TCP/IP model
- IP addressing IPv4 and IPv6
- Sub-netting
- Variable Length Subnet Masking (VLSM)
- VLANs and VTP
- Routing protocols and concepts

❖ Quiz

1. Which of the following are intermediary devices?
(Select all that apply.)

A. Router
B. Switch
C. Crossover cable
D. PCs

Answers: A, B

2. How many IP addresses can lease DHCP server?

A. 255
B. It is pool dependent.
C. 2^{48}
D. None

Answer: B

3. Which of the following is true regarding VTP?

A. VTP distributes VLAN configuration across the routers.
B. VTP distributes VLAN configuration across the switches.
C. VTP performs error correction over the trunk.

Answer: B

4. Which of the following commands delete VLANs from switch?

A. no vlan
B. erase vlans
C. delete flash:vlan.dat

Answer: C

5. What does the abbreviation RIP stand for?

A. Rest In Peace
B. Routing Information Protocol
C. Random Independent Packet.

Answer: B

6. Choose the correct cable for console connection between PC and router?

A. Rollover
B. Crossover
C. Pullover

Answer: A

"Intentionally blank"

PREPARING NETWORK FOR VOIP

CHAPTER 2

Chapter 2: PREPARING NETWORK FOR VOIP

The incorporation of VoIP to the existing network requires preparing the infrastructure. Network topology in our example consists of the minimum hardware components to accomplish the task and illustrates the basic configuration to prepare network for VoIP. Enterprise network is much more complex but it shares the same configuration patterns and approaches. Following pages do not explain every issue in depth, rather provide as much information as needed to clearly understand the matter. The primary step is to interconnect devices correctly and give them the names for the clear identification. Next steps ensure successful communication and IP addresses assignments. Following bullets summarize the scope of this chapter.

- ❖ Network topology scheme
- ❖ Hardware requirements
- ❖ Topology table
- ❖ Preparation and wiring of devices
- ❖ Hostnames
- ❖ VLANs and VTP
- ❖ DHCP
- ❖ The trunking
- ❖ Interfaces of routers
- ❖ The routing
- ❖ PCs
- ❖ Further study
- ❖ Show running-config
- ❖ Quiz

❖ Network topology scheme

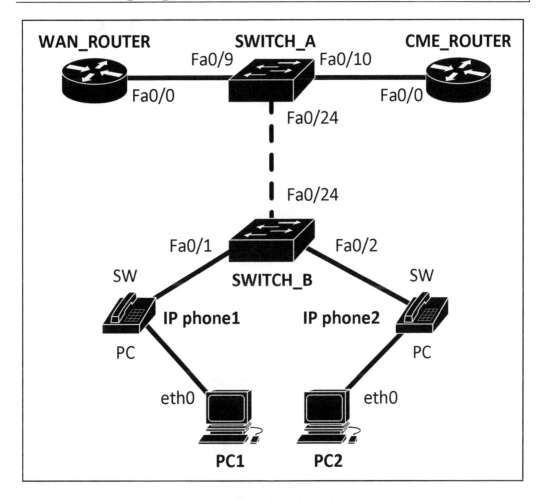

Figure 5: Network topology scheme

❖ Hardware requirements

2x Router (WAN_ROUTER, CME_ROUTER)
2x Switch (SWITCH_A, SWITCH_B)
2x IP phone (IP phone1, IP phone2)
2x PC (PC1, PC2)
6x Straight cable
1x Cross-over cable

❖ Topology table

Hostname	Interface	IP	Services
WAN_ROUTER	Fa0/0	*172.16.5.254/24*	DHCP Voice*172.16.1.10-250/24* DHCP Data *172.16.5.10-250/24*
CME_ROUTER	Fa0/0 Trunk	Fa0/0.1 *172.16.0.1/24*	ADMIN
		Fa0/0.10 *172.16.1.1/24*	VOICE CUCME
		Fa0/0.50 *172.16.5.1/24*	DATA
SWITCH_A	Fa0/9		access VLAN 5
	Fa0/10 Trunk		native VLAN 5
	Fa0/24 Trunk		native VLAN 5 allowed VLANs 5, 10, 50
SWITCH_B	Fa0/24 Trunk		native VLAN 5 allowed VLANs 5, 10, 50
	Range Fa0/1-6		PoE
PC1	Fa0	DHCP	
PC2	Fa0	DHCP	
IP phone1	SW, PC		
IP phone2	SW, PC		

Your notes:

❖ Preparation and wiring of devices

According to the topology scheme, two routers, two switches, two IP phones and PCs are required. If you are using CISCO intermediary devices, you should check the IOS version. Do not forget to erase startup-config and delete VLANs before you connect the device to the network. If you are using devices from different vendor, you should consult the documentation for proper configuration. Configuration directives and procedures may differ. The same applies to the IP phones. The procedure of IP phone integration and firmware registration is clearly explained in the following chapter. The procedure is similar for wide range of IP phone models. If you are using IP phones from different vendors, you should consult the documentation because the configuration directives and procedures may differ. PCs are required to have the Ethernet LAN adapter. Now we can start with the wiring. All the cables have to be connected to the correct ports. Do not forget to use cross-over cable to interconnect the switches. IP phones have multiple ports. We use the port labeled "SW" to connect IP phone to the SWITCH_B and the port labeled "PC" to connect PC.

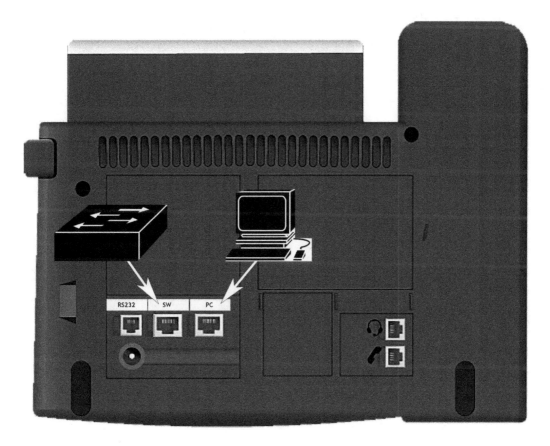

Figure 6: IP phone wiring

There are two possible ways how to power IP phone. The first one uses Alternate Current (AC) adapter with the power brick and the wall outlet. The second one requires PoE (Power over Ethernet) to power the IP phone. PoE is a technology that enables network cables carry electrical power together with data. In this case there is no need to use electrical outlets for end devices like IP phones and IP cameras. Main advantages of PoE are the time and the cost savings, flexibility, safety, reliability and scalability. PoE can be implemented directly by replacing non-PoE switches with PoE enabled switches. The PoE injector device can be used with non-PoE switches to implement a PoE without switch a replacement.

❖ Hostnames

The first reasonable configuration task is to set the hostnames of intermediary devices (routers and switches). We will configure multiple devices at once, and the hostname displayed in the console prevents us to configure an incorrect device by mistake.

SWITCH_A config (ch2c1):

```
Switch>enable
Switch#configure terminal
Switch(config)#hostname SWITCH_A
SWITCH_A(config)#exit
```

SWITCH_B config (ch2c2):

```
Switch>enable
Switch#configure terminal
Switch(config)#hostname SWITCH_B
SWITCH_B(config)#exit
```

WAN_ROUTER config (ch2c3):

```
Router>enable
Router#configure terminal
Router(config)#hostname WAN_ROUTER
WAN_ROUTER(config)#exit
```

CME_ROUTER config (ch2c4):

```
Router>enable
Router#configure terminal
Router(config)#hostname CME_ROUTER
CME_ROUTER(config)#exit
```

❖ VLANs and VTP

Because we have the voice integrated in same network as the data, the best practice is to make groups of hosts. At least two groups are created. One group is dedicated to the voice and second one to the data. In the process of grouping, hosts relocation and rewiring the links is one option. Of course, this option is probably not the best solution and sometimes nearly impossible. VLANs allow us to group the hosts together even if the hosts are not on the same network switch. VLAN membership can be configured through IOS on the switch or the router. We will configure three VLANs. VLAN 5 will serve the administrative purpose, VLAN 10 will deal with the voice and VLAN 50 will be devoted to data transfers.

SWITCH_A config (ch2c5):

```
SWITCH_A#configure terminal
SWITCH_A(config)#vlan 5
SWITCH_A(config-vlan)#name ADMIN
SWITCH_A(config-vlan)#exit
SWITCH_A(config)#vlan 10
SWITCH_A(config-vlan)#name VOICE
SWITCH_A(config-vlan)#exit
SWITCH_A(config)#vlan 50
SWITCH_A(config-vlan)#name DATA
SWITCH_A(config-vlan)#exit
SWITCH_A(config)#exit
```

This configuration has to be done on all the switches which carry the packets of created VLANs. If there are many switches in the network, manual configuration can be time consuming and it is easy to create inconsistency in configuration across the network. This can lead to nonfunctional network. Of course, there is an easy solution to this problem. VTP is a layer 2 messaging protocol that maintains VLAN configuration consistency by managing the addition, deletion, and renaming of VLANs within a VTP domain. One of the switches is designated as the server and all the VLAN modifications are made on the server switch. Client switches receive the current configuration from the server. We will configure SWITCH_A as a server for VTP domain VOICE and SWITCH_B as a client in the same VTP domain. Security plays an important role in this process, hence VTP password should be configured. The password must match across the same VTP domain. Now VLAN configuration we made on the SWITCH_A should be distributed across the VTP domain. [6]

SWITCH_A config (ch2c6):

```
SWITCH_A#configure terminal
SWITCH _A(config)#vtp mode server
SWITCH _A(config)#vtp domain VOICE
SWITCH _A(config)#vtp password SWi7ch69
SWITCH_A(config)#exit
```

SWITCH_B config (ch2c7):

```
SWITCH _B#configure terminal
SWITCH _B(config)#vtp mode client
SWITCH _B(config)#vtp domain VOICE
SWITCH _B(config)#vtp password SWi7ch69
SWITCH_B(config)#exit
```

❖ DHCP

DHCP is a configuration network protocol which distributes configuration parameters for example IP addresses. This considerably simplifies the administration of network. The protocol operates on the client-server model. Server creates pool of IP addresses which can be leased to clients. Clients use the broadcast to request an IP address from a server. DHCP server responds to their requests. Some ranges of IP addresses can also be excluded and they are not leased to the clients but serve the different purpose. The lease can be time limited and the IP address of a client has to be changed when the time period expires. DHCP can be also specified as a static, this means that the client gets the same IP address every time. In our configuration WAN_ROUTER takes the role of DHCP server. We need to specify separated DHCP pools for voice and data. Voice pool will include IP addresses for IP phones and data pool holds IP addresses for PCs.

WAN_ROUTER config (ch2c8):

```
WAN_ROUTER#configure terminal
WAN_ROUTER(config)#ip dhcp pool VOICE
WAN_ROUTER(dhcp-config)#network 172.16.1.0 255.255.255.0
WAN_ROUTER(dhcp-config)#default-router 172.16.1.1
WAN_ROUTER(dhcp-config)#option 150 ip 172.16.1.1
WAN_ROUTER(dhcp-config)#exit
WAN_ROUTER(config)#ip dhcp pool DATA
WAN_ROUTER(dhcp-config)#network 172.16.5.0 255.255.255.0
WAN_ROUTER(dhcp-config)#default-router 172.16.5.254
WAN_ROUTER(dhcp-config)#exit

WAN_ROUTER(config)#ip dhcp excluded-address 172.16.1.1 172.16.1.9
WAN_ROUTER(config)#ip dhcp excluded-address 172.16.5.1 172.16.5.9
WAN_ROUTER(config)#exit
```

Several other configuration parameters can be distributed with the DHCP. A default-router IP address provides the IP address of default gateway. A default gateway is the router which can forward packets to other networks. IP phones download their configuration from a Trivial File Transfer Protocol (TFTP) server. When a IP phone starts, if it does not have both the IP address and TFTP server IP address preconfigured, it sends a request with option 150 to the DHCP server to obtain this information. Option 150 specifies the IP address of TFTP server and needs to be configured on the DHCP server. In our case it is the IP address of CME_ROUTER. We can also exclude several addresses from both pools for different purpose. [3]

❖ The trunking

Trunk links are required to successfully transfer VLAN information between switches. A port on a switch is either an access port or a trunk port. An access port belongs to a single VLAN. An access port only carries traffic that comes from the VLAN assigned to the port. A trunk port is by default a member of all the VLANs that exist on the switch. It carries the traffic for all those VLANs. In our case we need to restrict a trunk to carry the traffic for VLANs 5, 10 and 50. The trunking has to be enabled on both sides of a link. Native VLAN frames are transmitted unchanged. Native VLAN is required by specific protocols to communicate over the trunk and it must match on both switches. [6]

SWITCH_A config (ch2c9):

```
SWITCH_A#configure terminal
SWITCH_A(config)#interface fa0/24
SWITCH_A(config-if)#switchport mode trunk
SWITCH_A(config-if)#switchport trunk native vlan 5
SWITCH_A(config-if)#switchport trunk allowed vlan 5,10,50
SWITCH_A(config-if)#exit

SWITCH_A(config)#interface fa0/9
SWITCH_A(config-if)#switchport mode access
SWITCH_A(config-if)#switchport access vlan 50
SWITCH_A(config-if)#exit

SWITCH_A(config)#interface fa0/10
SWITCH_A(config-if)#switchport mode trunk
SWITCH_A(config-if)#switchport trunk native vlan 5
SWITCH_A(config-if)#exit
SWITCH_A(config)#exit
```

Also port f0/10 on SWITCH_A is specified as a trunk even it is connected to the router. The purpose of this configuration will be explained later.

SWITCH_B config (ch2c10):

```
SWITCH_B#configure terminal
SWITCH_B(config)#interface fa0/24
SWITCH_B(config-if)#switchport mode trunk
SWITCH_B(config-if)#switchport trunk native vlan 5
SWITCH_B(config-if)#switchport trunk allowed vlan 5,10,50
SWITCH_B(config-if)#exit
SWITCH_B(config)#exit
```

We can use a port range to configure multiple ports at once. Ports fa0/1 and fa0/2 are connected to the IP phones and PCs. Ports will carry the traffic for VLAN 10 and VLAN 50. The *portfast* places ports in the forwarding state immediately. It will speed-up the process of IP phone registration.

SWITCH_B config (ch2c11):

```
SWITCH_B#configure terminal
SWITCH_B(config)#interface range fa0/1-6
SWITCH_B(config-if-range)#switchport mode access
SWITCH_B(config-if-range)#switchport voice vlan 10
SWITCH_B(config-if-range)#switchport access vlan 50
SWITCH_B(config-if-range)#spanning-tree portfast
SWITCH_B(config-if)#exit
SWITCH_B(config)#exit
```

❖ Interfaces of routers

WAN_ROUTER is designated as DHCP and Domain Name Server (DNS) for local network and also a default gateway for data VLAN. Interface fa0/0 needs to be configured with IP address 172.16.5.254/24.

WAN_ROUTER config (ch2c12):

```
WAN_ROUTER#configure terminal
WAN_ROUTER(config)#interface fa0/0
WAN_ROUTER(config-if)#ip address 172.16.5.254 255.255.255.0
WAN_ROUTER(config-if)#no shutdown
WAN_ROUTER(config-if)#exit
```

CME_ROUTER is configured as "Router on a stick". A single physical interface can be divided to the multiple logical sub-interfaces and CME_ROUTER router can provide inter-VLAN routing. We create sub-interface for each VLAN. Fa0/0.5 for administrative VLAN, fa0/0.10 for voice VLAN and fa0.50 for data VLAN. Encapsulation defines the encapsulation format in this case IEEE 802.1Q (dot1q).

CME_ROUTER config (ch2c13):

```
CME_ROUTER#configure terminal
CME_ROUTER(config)#interface fa0/0
CME_ROUTER(config-if)#no ip address
CME_ROUTER(config-if)#no shutdown
CME_ROUTER(config-if)#exit

CME_ROUTER(config)#interface fa0/0.5
CME_ROUTER(config-subif)#description INTERFACE FOR ADMIN VLAN
CME_ROUTER(config-subif)#encapsulation dot1q 5 native
CME_ROUTER(config-subif)#ip address 172.16.0.1 255.255.255.0
CME_ROUTER(config-subif)#no shutdown
CME_ROUTER(config-subif)#exit
CME_ROUTER(config)#interface fa0/0.10
CME_ROUTER(config-subif)#description INTERFACE FOR VOICE VLAN
CME_ROUTER(config-subif)#encapsulation dot1q 10
CME_ROUTER(config-subif)#ip address 172.16.1.1 255.255.255.0
```

```
CME_ROUTER(config-subif)#no shutdown
CME_ROUTER(config-subif)#exit

CME_ROUTER(config)#interface fa0/0.50
CME_ROUTER(config-subif)#description INTERFACE FOR DATA VLAN
CME_ROUTER(config-subif)#encapsulation dot1q 50
CME_ROUTER(config-subif)#ip address 172.16.5.1 255.255.255.0
CME_ROUTER(config-subif)#no shutdown
CME_ROUTER(config-subif)#exit

CME_ROUTER(config)#interface fa0/0.10
CME_ROUTER(config-subif)#ip helper-address 172.16.5.254
CME_ROUTER(config-subif)#exit
CME_ROUTER(config)#exit
```

When the IP phones broadcast request for an IP address from DHCP server, they broadcast on VLAN 10. Since the routers do not forward broadcasts, broadcast is terminated at the CME_ROUTER and does not reach the DHCP server on the WAN_ROUTER. *Helper-address* tells the interface to forward broadcast requests to the specified address. A solution is to configure *helper-address* on the CME_ROUTER sub-interface Fa0/0.10 to forward the DHCP requests to the WAN_ROUTER.

❖ The routing

Unfortunately, IP phones are not getting IP addresses form DHCP sever. The broadcast request now reaches the WAN_ROUTER but the response from WAN_ROUTER does not reach the IP phones. The routing needs to be configured. We use RIP version 2 for this purpose. [7]

CME_ROUTER config (ch2c14):

```
CME_ROUTER#configure terminal
CME_ROUTER(config)#router RIP
CME_ROUTER(config-router)#version 2
CME_ROUTER(config-router)#network 172.16.0.0
CME_ROUTER(config-router)#network 172.16.1.0
CME_ROUTER(config-router)#network 172.16.5.0
CME_ROUTER(config-router)#exit
CME_ROUTER(config)#exit
```

WAN_ROUTER config (ch2c15):

```
WAN_ROUTER#configure terminal
WAN_ROUTER(config)#router RIP
WAN_ROUTER(config-router)#version 2
WAN_ROUTER(config-router)#network 172.16.5.0
WAN_ROUTER(config-router)#exit
WAN_ROUTER(config)#exit
```

❖ PCs

PCs must have a DHCP enabled on the network adapter to get an IP address from the WAN_ROUTER. Windows PC DHCP configuration can be found under "Network connection menu" (Fig. 7). If we have multiple network adapters, be sure to choose the correct one. Double click on it, then click "Properties" and select "Internet Protocol Version 4". Make sure that "Obtain an IP address automatically" is selected.

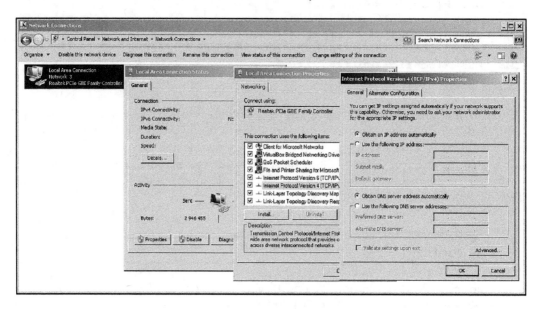

Figure 7: DHCP setting on Windows PC

Linux PCs require insert a few lines to the configuration files.

Debian-based distributions:

```
aptitude install dhcp-client

add following lines
auto eth0
iface eth0 inetdhcp
to this file
/etc/network/interfaces
```

Redhat-based distributions:

```
add following lines
DEVICE=eth0
BOOTPROTO=dhcp
ONBOOT=yes
to this file
/etc/sysconfig/network-scripts/ifcfg-eth0
```

If you have more than one network adapter, make sure you select the correct one (eth0, eth1...) [8]

❖ Further study

Further study advice for this chapter is almost identical with a previous chapter.

- Basic configuration of switch and router
- IP addressing IPv4 and IPv6
- Sub-netting
- Variable Length Subnet Masking (VLSM)
- VLANs and VTP
- Routing Information Protocol (RIP)
- IEEE 802.1Q (dot1q)

❖ Show running-config

SWITCH_A running-config:

```
hostname SWITCH_A
no aaa new-model
system mtu routing 1500
spanning-tree mode pvst
spanning-tree extend system-id
vlan internal allocation policy ascending
interface FastEthernet0/1
interface FastEthernet0/2
interface FastEthernet0/3
interface FastEthernet0/4
interface FastEthernet0/5
interface FastEthernet0/6
interface FastEthernet0/7
interface FastEthernet0/8
interface FastEthernet0/9
 switchport access vlan 50
 switchport mode access
interface FastEthernet0/10
 switchport trunk native vlan 5
 switchport mode trunk
interface FastEthernet0/11
interface FastEthernet0/12
interface FastEthernet0/13
interface FastEthernet0/14
interface FastEthernet0/15
interface FastEthernet0/16
interface FastEthernet0/17
interface FastEthernet0/18
interface FastEthernet0/19
interface FastEthernet0/20
interface FastEthernet0/21
interface FastEthernet0/22
interface FastEthernet0/23
interface FastEthernet0/24
 switchport trunk native vlan 5
 switchport trunk allowed vlan 5,10,50
 switchport mode trunk
interface GigabitEthernet0/1
interface GigabitEthernet0/2
interface Vlan1
 no ip address
no ip route-cache
 shutdown
ip http server
ip http secure-server
control-plane
line con 0
line vty 5 15
end
```

SWITCH_B running-config:

```
hostname SWITCH_B
no aaa new-model
system mtu routing 1500
ip subnet-zero
spanning-tree mode pvst
spanning-tree extend system-id
vlan internal allocation policy ascending
interface FastEthernet0/1
 switchport access vlan 50
 switchport mode access
 switchport voice vlan 10
 spanning-tree portfast
interface FastEthernet0/2
 switchport access vlan 50
 switchport mode access
 switchport voice vlan 10
 spanning-tree portfast
interface FastEthernet0/3
 switchport access vlan 50
 switchport mode access
 switchport voice vlan 10
 spanning-tree portfast
interface FastEthernet0/4
 switchport access vlan 50
 switchport mode access
 switchport voice vlan 10
 spanning-tree portfast
interface FastEthernet0/5
 switchport access vlan 50
 switchport mode access
 switchport voice vlan 10
 spanning-tree portfast
interface FastEthernet0/6
 switchport access vlan 50
 switchport mode access
 switchport voice vlan 10
 spanning-tree portfast
interface FastEthernet0/7
interface FastEthernet0/8
interface FastEthernet0/9
interface FastEthernet0/10
interface FastEthernet0/11
interface FastEthernet0/12
interface FastEthernet0/13
interface FastEthernet0/14
interface FastEthernet0/15
interface FastEthernet0/16
interface FastEthernet0/17
interface FastEthernet0/18
interface FastEthernet0/19
interface FastEthernet0/20
```

```
interface FastEthernet0/21
interface FastEthernet0/22
interface FastEthernet0/23
interface FastEthernet0/24
 switchport trunk native vlan 5
 switchport trunk allowed vlan 5,10,50
 switchport mode trunk
interface GigabitEthernet0/1
interface GigabitEthernet0/2
interface Vlan1
 no ip address
 no ip route-cache
ip http server
ip http secure-server
control-plane
line con 0
line vty 5 15
end
```

WAN_ROUTER running-config:

```
hostname WAN_ROUTER
no aaa new-model
memory-size iomem 25
ip cef
no ip dhcp use vrf connected
ip dhcp excluded-address 172.16.1.1 172.16.1.9
ip dhcp excluded-address 172.16.5.1 172.16.5.9
ip dhcp pool VOICE
   network 172.16.1.0 255.255.255.0
   default-router 172.16.1.1
   option 150 ip 172.16.1.1
ip dhcp pool DATA
   network 172.16.5.0 255.255.255.0
   default-router 172.16.5.254
ip auth-proxy max-nodata-conns 3
ip admission max-nodata-conns 3
voice-card 0
interface FastEthernet0/0
 ip address 172.16.5.254 255.255.255.0
 duplex auto
 speed auto
interface FastEthernet0/1
 no ip address
 shutdown
 duplex auto
 speed auto
interface Serial0/1/0
 no ip address
 shutdown
 no fair-queue
interface Serial0/1/1
```

```
 no ip address
 shutdown
 clock rate 125000
router rip
 version 2
 network 172.16.0.0
ip forward-protocol nd
ip http server
no ip http secure-server
control-plane
line con 0
line aux 0
line vty 0 4
 login
scheduler allocate 20000 1000
end
```

CME_ROUTER running-config:

```
hostname CME_ROUTER
no aaa new-model
memory-size iomem 25
dot11 syslog
ip source-route
ip cef
no ipv6 cef
multilink bundle-name authenticated
voice-card 0
license udi pid CISCO2811 sn FCZ123273T0
interface FastEthernet0/0
 no ip address
 duplex auto
 speed auto
interface FastEthernet0/0.5
 description ADMIN
 encapsulation dot1Q 5 native
 ip address 172.16.0.1 255.255.255.0
interface FastEthernet0/0.10
 description VOICE
 encapsulation dot1Q 10
 ip address 172.16.1.1 255.255.255.0
 ip helper-address 172.16.5.254
interface FastEthernet0/0.50
 description DATA
 encapsulation dot1Q 50
 ip address 172.16.5.1 255.255.255.0
interface FastEthernet0/1
 no ip address
 shutdown
 duplex auto
 speed auto
interface Serial0/0/0
```

```
 no ip address
 shutdown
 no fair-queue
 clock rate 125000
interface Serial0/0/1
 no ip address
 shutdown
interface Serial0/1/0
 no ip address
 shutdown
 clock rate 125000
interface Serial0/1/1
 no ip address
 shutdown
 clock rate 125000
router rip
 version 2
 network 172.16.0.0
ip forward-protocol nd
no ip http server
no ip http secure-server
control-plane
line con 0
line aux 0
line vty 0 4
 login
 transport input all
scheduler allocate 20000 1000
end
```

❖ Quiz

---

1. Which of the following methods are valid for powering a Cisco IP phone? (Select all that apply.)

    A. Power brick
    B. Crossover coupler
    C. PoE
    D. Using pins 1, 2, 3, and 4

    Answers: A, C

---

2. Which DHCP option provides the IP address of a TFTP server to a Cisco IP phone?

    A. Option 10
    B. Option 15
    C. Option 150
    D. Option 290

    Answer: C

---

3. Which of the following is true regarding VTP?

    A. All switches are VTP servers by default.
    B. All switches are VTP transparent by default.
    C. VTP is on by default with a domain name of Cisco on all Cisco switches.

    Answer: A

---

4. Which of the following commands sets a trunk port on switch?

    A. Trunk on
    B. Switchport trunk on
    C. Switchport mode trunk

    Answer: C

---

5. When a new trunk link is configured on an IOS-based switch, which VLANs are allowed over the link?

    A. By default, all VLANs are allowed on the trunk.
    B. No VLANs are allowed, you must configure each VLAN by hand.
    C. Only configured VLANs are allowed on the link.

    Answer: A

---

6. Which VTP mode allows you to change VLAN information on the switch?

    A. Client
    B. Transparent
    C. Server

    Answer: C

"Intentionally blank"

IP Phones SCCP

CHAPTER 3

A call between IP phones requires more than just connecting the phones to the network. This chapter summarizes the process of basic configuration of CUCME together with the IP phone registration procedure and a correct IP phone firmware selection and upload. An IP Communicator as the IP phone alternative is introduced as well. We use the topology and the basic configuration from the previous chapter.

- ❖ Basic CUCME SCCP configuration
- ❖ IP phone restart and reset procedure
- ❖ IP phone boot process and registration
- ❖ IP Communicator
- ❖ Further study
- ❖ Show running-config
- ❖ Quiz

❖ Basic CUCME SCCP configuration

CUCME is a call-processing software included in Cisco IOS. CUCME consists of the router that serves as a gateway and one or more VLANs that connect IP phones and phone devices to the router. At the moment, we present just minimal basic SCCP configuration to enable *telephony-service*. CUCME has an integrated guide, which we can use to configure basic parameters.

CME_ROUTER config (ch3c1):

```
CME_ROUTER#configure terminal
CME_ROUTER(config)#telephony-service setup

Do you want to start telephony-service setup? [yes/no]: y

Enter the IP source address for Cisco CallManager Express: 172.16.1.1

Enter the Skinny Port for Cisco CallManager Express:  [2000]:

How many IP phones do you want to configure : [0]: 10

What language do you want on IP phones?
     0  English
     ... Omitted output
 [0]:

Do you wish to change any of the above information? [yes/no]: no

CME_ROUTER(config-telephony)#exit
CME_ROUTER(config)#exit
```

To remove the entire CUCME configuration for IP phones, use the *no telephony-service* command. [9]

The same configuration of the basic parameters can be accomplished without the guide.

CME_ROUTER config (ch3c2):

```
CME_ROUTER#configure terminal
CME_ROUTER(config)#telephony-service
CME_ROUTER(config-telephony)#ip source-address 172.16.1.1 port
2000
CME_ROUTER(config-telephony)#max-ephones 10
CME_ROUTER(config-telephony)#max-dn 30
CME_ROUTER(config-telephony)#exit
CME_ROUTER(config)#exit
```

❖ IP phone restart and reset procedure

Complete the following steps to perform a factory reset of an IP phone:

- Unplug the PoE cable from the IP phone, and then plug in the cable again. The IP phone starts its power up cycle.
- Press and hold # button until the Headset, Mute, and Speaker buttons begin to flash in sequence, release #.
- Press 123456789*0# within 60 seconds after the Headset, Mute, and Speaker buttons begin to flash.
- If you enter this key sequence correctly, the IP phone goes through the factory reset process. [10]

CUCME allows you to reset and restart IP phones: [11]

Reset command:

- Similar to power-off, power-on reboot
- Downloads configurations for IP phones
- Contacts DHCP and TFTP servers for updated configuration
- Takes longer to process when updating multiple phones

Use *reset* command to complete the following tasks:

- Date and time settings
- Network locale
- Phone firmware
- Source address
- Voicemail access number
- Directory numbers
- Phone buttons

CME_ROUTER config (ch3c3):

```
Resets all IP phones

CME_ROUTER#configure terminal
CME_ROUTER(config)#telephony-service
CME_ROUTER(config-telephony)#reset all

Resets IP phone with the MAC address EFBF.311C.95CC

CME_ROUTER(config-telephony)#reset EFBF.311C.95CC
CME_ROUTER(config-telephony)#exit
CME_ROUTER(config)#exit
```

Restart command:

- Quick restart.
- Downloads configurations for IP phones.
- Phones contact the TFTP server for updated configuration information and reregister without contacting the DHCP server.
- Faster processing for multiple phones.

Use *restart* command to complete following tasks:

- Directory numbers
- Phone buttons
- Speed-dial numbers

CME_ROUTER config (ch3c4):

```
Restarts all IP phones

CME_ROUTER#configure terminal
CME_ROUTER(config)#telephony-service
CME_ROUTER(config-telephony)#restart all
CME_ROUTER(config-telephony)#exit
CME_ROUTER(config)#exit
```

❖ IP phone boot process and registration

After powering up, IP phone goes through the boot process.

- As the IP phone powers on, the switch delivers voice VLAN information to the IP phone using Cisco Discovery Protocol (CDP). The IP phone now knows voice VLAN.
- The IP phone broadcasts a DHCP request for an IP address on its voice VLAN.
- The DHCP server responds with an IP address. The IP phone receives the DHCP configuration. The DHCP configuration includes a default gateway, DNS and TFTP server.
- After the IP phone acquires the IP address of the TFTP server, it downloads a configuration file. It contains the list of valid call processing CUCME agents.
- The IP phone attempts to contact the primary call processing server to register. If this fails, the IP phone tries the next server in the configuration file. This process continues until the IP phone finds the active server or until the list of call processing agents is exhausted.
- If the IP phone finds an active server in the configuration file, it goes through the registration process using either the SCCP or SIP. Which protocol the IP phone uses is firmware dependent.
- Regardless of the protocol used, the IP phone contacts the server and identifies itself by its MAC address. The server checks the database and sends the operating

configuration to the IP phone. TFTP server configuration is the collection of basic settings, including items such as device language, firmware version, and more. The operating configuration is a different type of configuration and it contains directory or line numbers, ring tones and soft keys. The TFTP server configuration is sent, using the TFTP protocol and the operating configuration is sent, using SCCP or SIP.

- SCCP or SIP protocols are responsible for handling the majority of IP phones functions following the registration. [12]

IP phone may correctly operate right after we connect it and it is successfully registered. This means that IP phone firmware has been already downloaded by the IP phone. If we do the factory reset or IP phone does not have firmware loaded for some reason, it will display MAC address and the message "Upgrading". In this case, IP phone tries to download appropriate firmware files from TFTP server. If the files are there, IP phone will download and use them. If not, we need to upload them to the server and register them.

The following example illustrates how to upload and register IP phone firmware files. Firstly, we need to download appropriate files. SCCP and SIP firmware files for same type of IP phone differ, so we need to decide which protocol we will use. Search the IP phone vendor site for firmware files. Firmware files usually come in a compressed form like tar files. This compressed file includes multiple firmware files for IP phone. There is no need to decompress the file on your PC after the download. We will use TFTP to upload it to the CME_ROUTER and decompress it on the place. We will use the PC1 for this purpose. We need to check the IP address of the PC1. It was delivered by DHCP from WAN_ROUTER from DHCP data pool. One option is to use *ipconfig* in a command line window. The PC1 received IP address 172.16.5.10, your PC could and almost surely received a different IP address, but it has to be from the same DHCP data pool.

```
C:\Users\cisco>ipconfig

Windows IP Configuration


Ethernet adapter Ethernet:

   Connection-specific DNS Suffix  . :
   Link-local IPv6 Address . . . . . : fe80::18b3:3e67:c90:1438%3
   IPv4 Address. . . . . . . . . . . : 172.16.5.10
   Subnet Mask . . . . . . . . . . . : 255.255.255.0
   Default Gateway . . . . . . . . . : 172.16.5.254
```

Figure 8: PC IP configuration

Download and run TFTP software of your choice on the PC1. All we need to do is run the software and choose the directory where the tar firmware file is located. Also a correct network interface has to be selected. Now it is all set and ready.

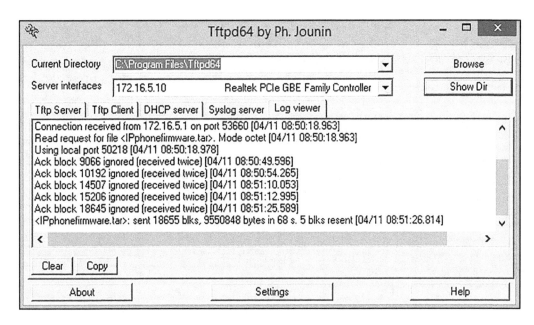

Figure 9: PC TFTP server [13]

We will use CME_ROUTER to download files from TFTP server that we already setup on the PC1. We need to check if PC1 is reachable from CME_ROUTER for a successful download. We use the ping command to accomplish that.

CME_ROUTER config (ch3c5):

```
CME_ROUTER#ping 172.16.5.10
Type escape sequence to abort.
Sending 5, 100-byte ICMP Echos to 172.16.5.10, timeout is 2 seconds:
.!!!!
Success rate is 100 percent (5/5), round-trip min/avg/max = 1/1/1 ms
```

PC1 is fully reachable and a download is possible. The following command downloads tar file from the PC1 and decompresses it on the router's flash card. Be careful with the tar file name. It must correspond with the name of firmware file located on the PC1. [14]

```
CME_ROUTER#archive tar /xtract
tftp://172.16.5.10/IPphonefirmware.tar flash:
Loading IPphonefirmware.tar from 172.16.5.10 (via FastEthernet0/0.50): !
extracting apps42.9-2-1TH1-13.sbn (4639974 bytes)!!!!!!!!!!!!!!!!!!!!
extracting cnu42.9-2-1TH1-13.sbn (575495 bytes)O!!
extracting cvm42sccp.9-2-1TH1-13.sbn (2208583 bytes)O!!!!!!!!!
extracting dsp42.9-2-1TH1-13.sbn (356907 bytes)O!
extracting jar42sccp.9-2-1TH1-13.sbn (1759967 bytes)!!!!!!!
extracting SCCP42.9-2-1S.loads (676 bytes)O
extracting term42.default.loads (680 bytes)
extracting term62.default.loads (680 bytes)
[OK - 9550848 bytes]
```

After a successful download all the files should be located on CME_ROUTER flash card. We can check it with the *show flash* command. Flash card contains IOS file and IP phone firmware files. Your flash card may contain many other files too and even firmware files names may differ. It depends on firmware version and IP phones types. We can possibly use other methods to transfer firmware files to the flash card. For example, we can use the card reader on PC. We remove the card from the router, insert it to the reader on PC, extract and copy the files directly to the card. Then insert it back to the router and we are good to go. However, this approach requires physical access to the router and may not be the best solution for the enterprise environment.

```
CME_ROUTER#show flash:
-#- --length-- -----date/time------ path
2            76 Sep 08 2015 11:35:42 System Volume Information/IndexerVolumeGuid
3      57726628 Oct 30 2009 11:37:36 Router IOS.bin
4       4639974 Nov 03 2015 13:56:34 apps42.9-2-1TH1-13.sbn
5        575495 Nov 03 2015 13:56:40 cnu42.9-2-1TH1-13.sbn
6       2208583 Nov 03 2015 13:56:54 cvm42sccp.9-2-1TH1-13.sbn
7        356907 Nov 03 2015 13:56:58 dsp42.9-2-1TH1-13.sbn
8       1759967 Nov 03 2015 13:57:10 jar42sccp.9-2-1TH1-13.sbn
9           676 Nov 03 2015 13:57:12 SCCP42.9-2-1S.loads
10          680 Nov 03 2015 13:57:12 term42.default.loads
11          680 Nov 03 2015 13:57:12 term62.default.loads

189669376 bytes available (67301376 bytes used)
```

All the downloaded files have to be registered with the TFTP server to be reachable for the IP phone. *Tftp-server* command allows us to register the files. Firmware, for different types of IP phones, uses different file names and the number of files also varies.

```
CME_ROUTER#configure terminal
CME_ROUTER(config)#tftp-server flash:apps42.9-2-1TH1-13.sbn
CME_ROUTER(config)#tftp-server flash:cnu42.9-2-1TH1-13.sbn
CME_ROUTER(config)#tftp-server flash:cvm42sccp.9-2-1TH1-13.sbn
CME_ROUTER(config)#tftp-server flash:dsp42.9-2-1TH1-13.sbn
CME_ROUTER(config)#tftp-server flash:jar42sccp.9-2-1TH1-13.sbn
CME_ROUTER(config)#tftp-server flash:SCCP42.9-2-1S.loads
CME_ROUTER(config)#tftp-server flash:term42.default.loads
CME_ROUTER(config)#tftp-server flash:term62.default.loads
```

After a successful TFTP registration, firmware needs to be associated with the specific type of IP phone. If we use *load* command followed by the question mark, console displays all the supported types. The group of supported types depends on which of IOS and CUCME is installed on the router. To build the eXtensible Markup Language (XML) configuration files that are required for IP phones in CUCME, we use the *create cnf-files* command. IP phone now should be able to download and install firmware. One specific type of the IP phone needs only one registration of firmware even if we use multiple phones of the same type in the network. If we include multiple types of IP phones, we need to complete the registration for each type separately. IP phone vendor download page provides you with convenient information which files you need to register and load in CUCME.

```
CME_ROUTER(config)#telephony-service
CME_ROUTER(config-telephony)#load ?
  12SP        12SP+ and 30VIP phones
  ... Omitted output
  7942        Cisco IP phone 7942
  7945        Cisco IP phone 7945
  7960-7940   Cisco IP phone 7940/7960
  7961        Cisco IP phone 7961
  7961GE      Cisco IP phone 7961GE
  7962        Cisco IP phone 7962
  7965        Cisco IP phone 7965
  7970        Cisco IP phone 7970
  7971        Cisco IP phone 7971
  7975        Cisco IP phone 7975
  7985        Cisco IP phone 7985
  ata         ATA  phone emulation for analog phone

CME_ROUTER(config-telephony)#load 7942 SCCP42.9-2-1S
CME_ROUTER(config-telephony)#create cnf-files
Creating CNF files...

CME_ROUTER(config-telephony)#exit
CME_ROUTER(config)#exit
```

To make a successfull call between IP phones, we need to register the phones and create associations with the call numbers. An ephone-dn (Ethernet phone directory number) represents the line that connects a voice channel to IP phone, on which a user can receive and make calls. An ephone-dn has one or more extensions or telephone numbers associated with it. An ephone-dn is equivalent to a phone line in most cases. Each ephone-dn has a unique dn-tag or a sequence number to identify it during configuration. In our configuration we create two ephone-dns, one for each IP phone. [15]

CME_ROUTER config (ch3c6):

```
CME_ROUTER#configure terminal
CME_ROUTER(config)#ephone-dn ?
<1-150>   ephone-dn tag
CME_ROUTER(config)#ephone-dn 1
CME_ROUTER(config-ephone-dn)#number 1001
CME_ROUTER(config-ephone-dn)#exit
CME_ROUTER(config)#ephone-dn 2
CME_ROUTER(config-ephone-dn)#number 1002
CME_ROUTER(config-ephone-dn)#exit
CME_ROUTER(config)#exit
```

An ephone (Ethernet phone) is a single logical instance associated with the physical phone. The physical ephone is either IP phone or an analog telephone adaptor with an attached analog phone or fax. *Show ephone* command displays the basic information about registered ephones. We will use the unique MAC address of ephone to register a physical phone and to associate ephone-dn with it.

CME_ROUTER config (ch3c7):

```
CME_ROUTER#show ephone
ephone-1[0] Mac:10BD.0000.0001 TCP socket:[1] activeLine:0 whisperLine:0
REGISTERED in SCCP ver 20/12 max_streams=5
mediaActive:0 whisper_mediaActive:0 startMedia:0 offhook:0 ringing:0 reset:0
reset_sent:0 paging 0 debug:0 caps:9
IP:172.16.1.13 49611 7942  keepalive 41 max_line 2 available_line 2
Preferred Codec: g711ulaw

ephone-2[1] Mac:10BD.0000.0002 TCP socket:[2] activeLine:0 whisperLine:0
REGISTERED in SCCP ver 20/12 max_streams=5
mediaActive:0 whisper_mediaActive:0 startMedia:0 offhook:0 ringing:0 reset:0
reset_sent:0 paging 0 debug:0 caps:9
IP:172.16.1.12 52557 7942  keepalive 41 max_line 2 available_line 2
Preferred Codec: g711ulaw
```

The following configuration registers physical IP phone (MAC address 10BD.0000.0001) as ephone 1 and assigns ephone-dn 1 to its button 1. IP phone (MAC address 10BD.0000.0002) is registered as ephone 2 and ephone-dn 2 is assigned to its button 1.

```
CME_ROUTER#configure terminal
CME_ROUTER(config)#ephone 1
CME_ROUTER(config-ephone)#mac-address 10BD.0000.0001
CME_ROUTER(config-ephone)#button 1:1
CME_ROUTER(config-ephone)#exit

CME_ROUTER(config)#ephone 2
CME_ROUTER(config-ephone)#mac-address 10BD.0000.0002
CME_ROUTER(config-ephone)#button 1:2
CME_ROUTER(config-ephone)#exit

CME_ROUTER(config)#telephony-service
CME_ROUTER(config-telephony)#reset all
CME_ROUTER(config)#exit
```

The correct registration can be reviewed as follows. We check the functionality by dialing the 1002 on the IP phone 1. IP phone 2 (number 1002) should ring and/or flash in sequence. Buttons and assigned ephone-dns can be also displayed with *show ephone* command.

```
CME_ROUTER#show ephone
ephone-1[0] Mac:10BD.0000.0001 TCP socket:[1] activeLine:0 whisperLine:0
REGISTERED in SCCP ver 20/12 max_streams=5
mediaActive:0 whisper_mediaActive:0 startMedia:0 offhook:0 ringing:0 reset:0
reset_sent:0 paging 0 debug:0 caps:9
IP:172.16.1.13 50539 7942  keepalive 1 max_line 2 available_line 2
button 1: dn 1  number 1001 CH1    IDLE
Preferred Codec: g711ulaw

ephone-2[1] Mac:10BD.0000.0002 TCP socket:[2] activeLine:0 whisperLine:0
REGISTERED in SCCP ver 20/12 max_streams=5
mediaActive:0 whisper_mediaActive:0 startMedia:0 offhook:0 ringing:0 reset:0
reset_sent:0 paging 0 debug:0 caps:9
IP:172.16.1.12 50424 7942  keepalive 1 max_line 2 available_line 2
button 1: dn 2  number 1002 CH1    IDLE
Preferred Codec: g711ulaw
```

Deregistration of an ephone, ephone-dn and buttons is possible with no form of commands. The following example shows the deregistration of ephones 1 and 2.

```
CME_ROUTER#configure terminal
CME_ROUTER(config)#no ephone 1
*Nov  4 10:19:40.831: %IPPHONE-6-UNREGISTER_NORMAL: ephone-1:SEP10BD.0000.0001
IP:172.16.1.13 Socket:1 DeviceType:Phone has unregistered normally.

CME_ROUTER(config)#no ephone 2
*Nov  4 10:20:16.343: %IPPHONE-6-UNREGISTER_NORMAL: ephone-2:SEP10BD.0000.0002
IP:172.16.1.12 Socket:2 DeviceType:Phone has unregistered normally.

CME_ROUTER(config)#
*Nov  4 10:20:33.951: %IPPHONE-6-REGISTER_NEW: ephone-1:SEP10BD.0000.0001
IP:172.16.1.13 Socket:1 DeviceType:Phone has registered.
*Nov  4 10:21:09.923: %IPPHONE-6-REGISTER_NEW: ephone-2:SEP10BD.0000.0002
IP:172.16.1.12 Socket:2 DeviceType:Phone has registered.

CME_ROUTER(config)#exit
```

Because the automatic registration of ephones is enabled by default, both phones automatically register again. CUCME allocates an ephone slot to any ephone that connects to it. The *no auto-reg-ephone* command blocks the automatic registration of ephones whose MAC addresses are not included in the configuration. Blocked registration ephone attempts can be displayed with the *attempted-registrations* command.

```
CME_ROUTER#configure terminal
CME_ROUTER(config)#telephony-service
CME_ROUTER(config-telephony)#no auto-reg-ephone
CME_ROUTER(config)#exit
```

Do not forget to turn auto registration back on and register IP phones 1 and 2 to successfully complete this chapter.

❖ IP Communicator

Cisco IP Communicator is a desktop based IP phone application. With microphone and headphones connected to the PC, IP Communicator can operate as an ordinary IP phone with CUCME. The only thing we need to configure in IP Communicator's preferences is an IP address of TFTP server. All the other configuration settings are not essential for IP Communicator CUCME registration. We use TFTP IP address 172.16.1.1. The process of assigning ephone-dns to the buttons is the same as for an ordinary IP phone. This task requires administrator account. [16]

Figure 10: CISCO IP Communicator

❖ Further study

Further study of the following subjects is strongly advised.

- SCCP
- CUCME SCCP overview
- TFTP

❖ Show running-config

CME_ROUTER running-config:

```
hostname CME_ROUTER
no aaa new-model
dot11 syslog
ip source-route
ip cef
no ipv6 cef
multilink bundle-name authenticated
voice-card 0
interface FastEthernet0/0
 no ip address
 duplex auto
 speed auto
interface FastEthernet0/0.5
 description ADMIN
 encapsulation dot1Q 5 native
 ip address 172.16.0.1 255.255.255.0
interface FastEthernet0/0.10
 description VOICE
 encapsulation dot1Q 10
 ip address 172.16.1.1 255.255.255.0
 ip helper-address 172.16.5.254
interface FastEthernet0/0.50
 description DATA
 encapsulation dot1Q 50
 ip address 172.16.5.1 255.255.255.0
interface FastEthernet0/1
 no ip address
 shutdown
 duplex auto
 speed auto
interface Serial0/0/0
 no ip address
 shutdown
 no fair-queue
 clock rate 125000
interface Serial0/0/1
```

```
 no ip address
 shutdown
 clock rate 125000
interface Serial0/1/0
 no ip address
 shutdown
 clock rate 125000
interface Serial0/1/1
 no ip address
 shutdown
 clock rate 125000
router rip
 version 2
 network 172.16.0.0
ip forward-protocol nd
no ip http server
no ip http secure-server
control-plane
telephony-service
 max-ephones 10
 max-dn 30
 ip source-address 172.16.1.1 port 2000
 max-conferences 8 gain -6
 transfer-system full-consult
 create cnf-files version-stamp Jan 01 2002 00:00:00
ephone-dn  1
 number 1001
ephone-dn  2
 number 1002
ephone  1
 device-security-mode none
 mac-address 10BD.0000.0001
 button  1:1
ephone  2
 device-security-mode none
 mac-address 10BD.0000.0002
 button  1:2
line con 0
line aux 0
line vty 0 4
 login
scheduler allocate 20000 1000
end
```

❖ Quiz

1. Which of the following signaling methods can CUCME use for endpoint control? (Choose two.)

   A. SCCP
   B. SIP
   C. H.632
   D. MGCD

   Answers: A, B

---

2. Two users are talking on IP phones to each other in the same office. Through the call, an administrator reboots the CUCME router. What happens to the current call?

   A. The call is immediately terminated.
   B. CUCME router won't boot again.
   C. The call remains active.
   D. The call is on hold.

   Answer: C

---

3. What type of compressed archive can you download from Cisco to reinstall all support files?

   A. TAR file
   B. ZIP file
   C. GZ file
   D. RAR file

   Answer: A

---

4. Which file will be sent to un-configured Cisco IP phone by TFTP?

   A. XMLDefault.cnf.xml
   B. Firmware.xmf
   C. MAC address copy
   D. None

   Answer: A

---

5. You want to assign the directory number 1005 to the second line button on IP phone. Choose the correct answer.

   A. button 2<->1005
   B. button 1:2:3:1005
   C. button 1005:2
   D. button 2:1005
   E. button /dev/null

   Answer: D

"Intentionally blank"

BASIC CONFIGURATION SCCP

CHAPTER 4

Chapter 4: BASIC CONFIGURATION SCCP

The following chapter presents the basic CUCME configuration of directory numbers, ephones and system settings that are essential for more advanced setup. We will explain how to assign directory numbers and how to overcome multiple problems which may appear as a configuration develops into more complex scenario.

- ❖ Directory numbers and buttons
- ❖ Shared line
- ❖ Button overlays
- ❖ Auto assign
- ❖ Ephone-dn template
- ❖ Time and date
- ❖ Description, name and label
- ❖ System message
- ❖ Further study
- ❖ Quiz

❖ Directory numbers and buttons

The initial topology and configuration of the network for this chapter stays the same as in the previous chapters. We additionally connect four more IP phones to the SWITCH_B, ports fa0/3-6. Total number of six IP phones allows us to test more complex scenarios. In case we use previous configurations, we need to wipe clean telephony service configuration on CME_ROUTER. *No telephony-service* command is the best option for this task. We also need to re-enable telephony service and configure the basic parameters as follows.

CME_ROUTER config (ch4c1):

```
CME_ROUTER#configure terminal
CME_ROUTER(config)#no telephony-service

CME_ROUTER(config)#telephony-service
CME_ROUTER(config-telephony)#ip source-address 172.16.1.1 port
2000
CME_ROUTER(config-telephony)#max-ephones 10
CME_ROUTER(config-telephony)#max-dn 30
CME_ROUTER(config-telephony)#exit
CME_ROUTER(config)#exit
```

Initially, we will use three ephone-dns. The first one is configured as a default single-line directory number. The second one uses the dual-line directory number. And the last one has two numbers assigned. With a single-line directory number the ephone-dn is only able to make or receive one call at the time. If another call arrives on busy ephone-dn, the caller will receive a busy signal. A dual-line directory number is able to handle two simultaneous calls. This is useful for supporting features such as call waiting, conference calling and consultative transfers, but is not appropriate for voice-mail numbers, intercoms or ephone-dns used for message-waiting indicators, paging, loopback, or hunt groups. An octo-line directory number supports up to eight active calls, both incoming and outgoing, on a single phone button. Secondary number enables the ephone-dn to answer multiple numbers. For example, an extension can be reached by dialing the four digit internal network number or full Public Switched Telephone Network (PSTN) number.

CME_ROUTER config (ch4c2):

```
CME_ROUTER#configure terminal
CME_ROUTER(config)#ephone-dn 1
CME_ROUTER(config-ephone-dn)#number 1001
CME_ROUTER(config-ephone-dn)#exit

CME_ROUTER(config)#ephone-dn 2 dual-line
CME_ROUTER(config-ephone-dn)#number 1002
CME_ROUTER(config-ephone-dn)#exit

CME_ROUTER(config)#ephone-dn 3
CME_ROUTER(config-ephone-dn)#number 1003 secondary 44555003
CME_ROUTER(config-ephone-dn)#exit
CME_ROUTER(config)#exit
```

The following example shows advanced assignment of ephone-dns to the buttons. Each ephone has the first and the second button linked with ephone-dns. Separator ":" is used to link a directory number with the button. There are also alternative separators like "S, b, f, m". These separators also assign ephone-dn to the button, but the IP phone handles incoming call differently. [17]

CME_ROUTER config (ch4c3):

```
CME_ROUTER#configure terminal
CME_ROUTER(config)#ephone 1
CME_ROUTER(config-ephone)#mac-address 10BD.0000.0001
CME_ROUTER(config-ephone)#button 1:1 2S3
CME_ROUTER(config-ephone)#exit

CME_ROUTER(config)#ephone 2
CME_ROUTER(config-ephone)#mac-address 10BD.0000.0002
CME_ROUTER(config-ephone)#button 1:2 2b1
CME_ROUTER#configure terminal

CME_ROUTER(config)#ephone 3
CME_ROUTER(config-ephone)#mac-address 10BD.0000.0003
CME_ROUTER(config-ephone)#button 1f3
CME_ROUTER(config-ephone)#button 2m2
CME_ROUTER(config-ephone)#exit

CME_ROUTER(config)#telephony-service
CME_ROUTER(config-telephony)#reset all
CME_ROUTER(config-telephony)#exit
CME_ROUTER(config)#exit
```

Separators:

"`:`" Ordinary ring. The IP phone rings and flashes normally on incoming call.

"b" Call waiting beep, no ring. The IP phone ringer is suppressed on incoming call, but the handset light flashes. Call waiting beeps are active during active calls.

"f" Feature ring. The IP phone performs a triple ring on incoming calls.

"m" Monitor mode. The IP phone does not ring for incoming calls and it is unable to place outgoing calls. It simply monitors the status of a shared line.

"o" Overlay line (no call waiting). Overlay lines are used to create a shared-line experience between multiple ephones.

"c" Overlay line (with call waiting). It is the same as "o", but call waiting is active.

"x" Overlay expansion/rollover. It allows calls to roll over to additional lines of the IP phone when all other overlay lines are busy.

"S" Silent ring. It disables ring and call waiting beep for incoming calls. The lights are active.

"w" Watch mode. It is the same as "m", but watches all the lines on the phone for which the watched line is the primary. [18]

Here are a few test scenarios for new configuration:

No. 1	dial	headset	ring	button 1	button 2
ephone 1		flashes red	rings	flashes orange	red
ephone 2		off	off	off	flashes orange
ephone 3	1001	off	dial tone	green	off

No. 2	dial	headset	ring	button 1	button 2
ephone 1		off	off	off	flashes orange
ephone 2	1003	off	dial tone	green	off
ephone 3		flashes red	triple ring	flashes orange	red

No. 3	dial	headset	ring	button 1	button 2
ephone 1	1002	off	dial tone	green	off
ephone 2		flashes red	rings	flashes orange	red
ephone 3		off	off	off	red

❖ Shared line

We can create the shared line by assigning the same ephone-dn to the multiple ephones. The same directory numbers display on multiple IP phones. An incoming call to number 1111 will ring on ephone 4 and 5 simultaneously. Whichever IP phone answers first it gets the call. The problem is that only one call can use shared line at the time. The rest of the IP phones display the shared line as if it were in use.

CME_ROUTER config (ch4c4):

```
CME_ROUTER#configure terminal
CME_ROUTER(config)#ephone-dn 11 dual-line
CME_ROUTER(config-ephone-dn)#number 1111
CME_ROUTER(config-ephone-dn)#exit

CME_ROUTER(config)#ephone 4
CME_ROUTER(config-ephone)#mac-address 10BD.0000.0004
CME_ROUTER(config-ephone)#button 1:11
CME_ROUTER(config-ephone)#restart
CME_ROUTER(config-ephone)#exit

CME_ROUTER(config)#ephone 5
CME_ROUTER(config-ephone)#mac-address 10BD.0000.0005
CME_ROUTER(config-ephone)#button 1:11
CME_ROUTER(config-ephone)#restart
CME_ROUTER{config-ephone)#exit
CME_ROUTER{config)#exit
```

We can test this scenario by dialing the directory number 1111 on ephone 1.

No. 1	dial	headset	ring	button 1	button 2
ephone 1	1111	off	dial tone	green	off
ephone 4	✕	flashes red	rings	flashes orange	off
ephone 5	✕	flashes red	rings	flashes orange	off

We answer the call on ephone 4 and keep the call active. Dial the directory number 1111 on ephone 2.

No. 2	dial	headset	ring	button 1	button 2
ephone 2	1111	off	dial tone	green	off
ephone 1	in call	active	off	green	off
ephone 4	✕	off	off	green	off
ephone 5	✕	off	off	red	off

A problem with single directory number shared among the multiple ephones can be solved by assigning the same directory number to the multiple ephone-dns.

CME_ROUTER config (ch4c5):

```
CME_ROUTER#configure terminal
CME_ROUTER(config)#ephone-dn 12 dual-line
CME_ROUTER(config-ephone-dn)#number 1111
CME_ROUTER(config-ephone-dn)#exit

CME_ROUTER(config)#no ephone 4
CME_ROUTER(config)#ephone 4
CME_ROUTER(config-ephone)#mac-address 10BD.0000.0004
CME_ROUTER(config-ephone)#button 1:11
CME_ROUTER(config-ephone)#restart
CME_ROUTER(config-ephone)#exit

CME_ROUTER(config)#no ephone 5
CME_ROUTER(config)#ephone 5
CME_ROUTER(config-ephone)#mac-address 10BD.0000.0005
CME_ROUTER(config-ephone)#button 1:12
CME_ROUTER(config-ephone)#restart
CME_ROUTER{config-ephone)#exit
CME_ROUTER{config)#exit
```

Now we can test the same scenario by dialing the directory number 1111 on ephone 1.

No. 1	dial	headset	ring	button 1	button 2
ephone 1	1111	off	dial tone	green	off
ephone 4	✕	flashes red	rings	flashes orange	off
ephone 5	✕	off	off	off	off

We answer the call on ephone 4 and keep the call active. Dial the directory number 1111 on ephone 2.

No. 2	dial	headset	ring	button 1	button 2
ephone 2	1111	off	dial tone	green	off
ephone 1	in call	active	off	green	off
ephone 4		active	off	green	off
ephone 5		flashes red	rings	flashes orange	off

We are now able to reach both ephones 4 and 5 calling the same directory number, however, another problem appears. When the CME_ROUTER receives the call for 1111, it has to choose from multiple equal ephone-dns to deliver the call. In this case the pick is completely random. Sometimes ephone 4 gets the call, sometimes it is ephone 5. We can test this by placing and ending the multiple calls to the directory number 1111 form ephone 1. We can gain control over how the call is delivered with the use of *preference* command. We can assign preference value from 0 to 10, were lower values represent higher priority. Preference 0 is default value.

CME_ROUTER config (ch4c6):

```
CME_ROUTER#configure terminal
CME_ROUTER(config)#ephone-dn 11
CME_ROUTER(config-ephone-dn)#preference 5
CME_ROUTER(config-ephone-dn)#exit

CME_ROUTER(config)#ephone-dn 12
CME_ROUTER(config-ephone-dn)#preference 1
CME_ROUTER(config-ephone-dn)#exit
CME_ROUTER(config)#exit
```

With this configuration, the primary call to the directory number 1111 is always delivered to the ephone 5. Ephone-dns 11 and 12 are configured as dual-line. It enables them to handle multiple incoming and outgoing calls. Secondary incoming call to 1111, with primary call still active will not roll over to ephone-dn 11, instead it will be received via call waiting on ephne-dn 12. This situation can be handled with *huntstop* command. *Huntstop* command has two forms. Standalone *huntstop* prevents CME_ROUTER from hunting for another directory number match. And *huntstop channel* tells the CME_ROUTER to stop hunting for other channel on the same IP phone. [19]

CME_ROUTER config (ch4c7):

```
CME_ROUTER#configure terminal
CME_ROUTER(config)#ephone-dn 11
CME_ROUTER(config-ephone-dn)#huntstop channel
CME_ROUTER(config-ephone-dn)#exit
CME_ROUTER(config)#ephone-dn 12
CME_ROUTER(config-ephone-dn)#huntstop channel
CME_ROUTER(config-ephone-dn)#no huntstop
CME_ROUTER(config-ephone-dn)#exit
CME_ROUTER(config)#exit
```

Now, the primary call to directory number 1111 is delivered to ephone 5. If primary call is answered, secondary call to directory number is delivered to the ephone 4. All the other calls to directory number 1111 will receive a busy signal.

❖ Button overlays

The main reason to use the overlays is to overcome the limited number of physical buttons available on an IP phone. The key to this configuration is the "o" or "c" separator. In the following example, a simple overlay button is created.

"o"   creates an overlay set without call waiting
"c"   creates an overlay set with call waiting
"x"   creates an overlay rollover expansion button - for use when a primary overlay button is occupied with a call instead of using call waiting. (It does not work with "c") [19]

CME_ROUTER config (ch4c8):

```
CME_ROUTER#configure terminal
CME_ROUTER(config)#ephone-dn 14
CME_ROUTER(config-ephone-dn)#number 1014
CME_ROUTER(config-ephone-dn)#exit

CME_ROUTER(config)#ephone-dn 15
CME_ROUTER(config-ephone-dn)#number 1015
CME_ROUTER(config-ephone-dn)#exit

CME_ROUTER(config)#ephone 6
CME_ROUTER(config-ephone)#mac-address 10BD.0000.0006
CME_ROUTER(config-ephone)#button 1o14,15
CME_ROUTER(config-ephone)#button 2x1
CME_ROUTER(config-ephone)#exit
CME_ROUTER(config)#exit
```

Ephone 6 has now two ephone-dns assigned to the first button. It can be reached by dialing both 1014 and 1015 directory numbers. If we dial 1014 on ephone 1, ephone 6 rings and we can answer the call. We answer the call and leave it active. Dial 1014 on ephone 2. Ephone 2 receives the busy signal. It is because we configured ephone-dn 14 as the single-line. If we try to dial 1015 on ephone 2 with the call from ephone 1 still active, we receive a dial tone. If we use "o" separator, an incoming call from ephone 2 is not displayed on ephone 6. Thanks to "x" separator, a call from ephone 2 will roll over to button 2. Command *button 2x1* does not associate button 2 with ephone-dn 1, rather it allows button 2 to be an overflow button of button 1. "x" separator cannot be obviously combined with "c" separator. If we want to be able to see the second call on ephone 4, we need to use separator "c" instead of "o". We leave both calls from ephone 1 and ephone 2 active. If we try to dial directory number 1014 or 1015 from ephone 3, we get the busy signal for both numbers. The situation with dual-line directory numbers requires the use of *preference* and *huntstop* command as it was already presented.

There is also a possibility to combine shared lines with the button overlays. Initially, we need to remove all the ephones and ephone-dns.

CME_ROUTER config (ch4c9):

```
CME_ROUTER#configure terminal
CME_ROUTER(config)#no telephony-service

CME_ROUTER(config)#telephony-service
CME_ROUTER(config-telephony)#ip source-address 172.16.1.1 port
2000
CME_ROUTER(config-telephony)#max-ephones 10
CME_ROUTER(config-telephony)#max-dn 30
CME_ROUTER(config-telephony)#exit
CME_ROUTER(config)#exit
```

Directory numbers 11 and 12 are configured with the shared line number 1111. Directory numbers 21 through 23 do not share the line. Each one has a unique number.

```
CME_ROUTER#configure terminal
CME_ROUTER(config)#ephone-dn 11 dual-line
CME_ROUTER(config-ephone-dn)#number 1111
CME_ROUTER(config-ephone-dn)#preference 0
CME_ROUTER(config-ephone-dn)#huntstop channel
CME_ROUTER(config-ephone-dn)#no hunstop
CME_ROUTER(config-ephone-dn)#exit

CME_ROUTER(config)#ephone-dn 12 dual-line
CME_ROUTER(config-ephone-dn)#number 1111
CME_ROUTER(config-ephone-dn)#preference 1
CME_ROUTER(config-ephone-dn)#huntstop channel
CME_ROUTER(config-ephone-dn)#exit

CME_ROUTER(config)#ephone-dn 21
CME_ROUTER(config-ephone-dn)#number 1021
CME_ROUTER(config-ephone-dn)#exit

CME_ROUTER(config)#ephone-dn 22
CME_ROUTER(config-ephone-dn)#number 1022
CME_ROUTER(config-ephone-dn)#exit

CME_ROUTER(config)#ephone-dn 23
CME_ROUTER(config-ephone-dn)#number 1023
CME_ROUTER(config-ephone-dn)#exit
CME_ROUTER(config)#exit
```

We use different ephones numbering this time. Ephones 11 and 12 have directory numbers 11 and 12 assigned to the first button as the overlay. Ephones 21, 22 and 23 have directory numbers 21, 22 and 23 assigned correspondingly. This is typical "Support service" configuration. Ephones 11 and 12 will serve as IP phones for employees of the support team and ephones 21, 22 and 23 as the customer callers. The first customer's call will be sent to all support phones. The call can be answered on any of these phones by the support employee. With the first call still active, the following calls are delivered to the other support phones that are still free. If all the support phones are in active call, another customer receives the busy signal. We use only two support phones to demonstrate the situation. Of course, the more support phones we have the more customer calls we can handle.

```
CME_ROUTER#configure terminal
CME_ROUTER(config)#ephone 11
CME_ROUTER(config-ephone)#mac-address 10BD.0000.0001
CME_ROUTER(config-ephone)#button 1o11,12
CME_ROUTER(config-ephone)#restart
CME_ROUTER(config-ephone)#exit

CME_ROUTER(config)#ephone 12
CME_ROUTER(config-ephone)#mac-address 10BD.0000.0002
CME_ROUTER(config-ephone)#button 1o11,12
CME_ROUTER(config-ephone)#restart
CME_ROUTER(config-ephone)#exit
CME_ROUTER(config)#exit

CME_ROUTER(config)#ephone 21
CME_ROUTER(config-ephone)#mac-address 10BD.0000.0003
CME_ROUTER(config-ephone)#button 1:21
CME_ROUTER(config-ephone)#restart
CME_ROUTER(config-ephone)#exit

CME_ROUTER(config)#ephone 22
CME_ROUTER(config-ephone)#mac-address 10BD.0000.0004
CME_ROUTER(config-ephone)#button 1:22
CME_ROUTER(config-ephone)#restart
CME_ROUTER(config-ephone)#exit

CME_ROUTER(config)#ephone 23
CME_ROUTER(config-ephone)#mac-address 10BD.0000.0005
CME_ROUTER(config-ephone)#button 1:23
CME_ROUTER(config-ephone)#restart
CME_ROUTER(config-ephone)#exit
CME_ROUTER(config)#exit
```

❖ Auto assign

Auto assign creates an ephone configuration for IP phone whose MAC address is not explicitly configured. The *auto-reg-ephone* command must be enabled (enabled by default) to use auto assign. The *auto assign* command cannot create shared lines. We can use multiple *auto assign* commands to assign discontinuous ranges of ephone-dns to the different types of IP phones. If no type parameter is specified, ephone-dns are assigned to any type of IP phones. [20]

CME_ROUTER config (ch4c10):

```
CME_ROUTER#configure terminal

CME_ROUTER(config)#no ephone 21
CME_ROUTER(config)#no ephone 22
CME_ROUTER(config)#no ephone 23

CME_ROUTER(config)# telephony-service
CME_ROUTER(config-telephony)# auto assign 21 to 23 type ?
WORD  7960, 7940, 7910, 7905, 7906, 7935, 7902, 7911, 7912,
7961, 7961E, 7941, 7941GE, 7920, 7921, 7970, 7971, 7936, 7931, CIPC,7962, 7942,
7945, 7965, 7975, 7985, anl or bri

CME_ROUTER(config-telephony)#auto assign 21 to 23
CME_ROUTER(config-telephony)#restart all
CME_ROUTER(config-telephony)#exit
CME_ROUTER(config)#exit
```

❖ Ephone-dn template

We can quickly pass multiple configuration parameters to the IP phone by creating the ephone template. The template can be subsequently applied to the multiple ephones using the *ephone-template* command in ephone configuration mode. We can define multiple different ephone templates, but we cannot apply more than one template to single ephone. The following example illustrates the use of ephone-template command to modify the order of soft keys. [21]

CME_ROUTER config (ch4c11):

```
CME_ROUTER#configure terminal
CME_ROUTER(config)#ephone-template 6
CME_ROUTER(config-ephone-template)#?

Ephone template configuration commands:
after-hours             define after-hours patterns, date, etc
block-blind-xf-fallback No fallback to blind transfer if consult transfer
                          failed
busy-trigger-per-button Define the number of calls that triggers call
                          forward busy per octo-line button of this ephone
button-layout           Button layout format for phone
codec                   Set preferred codec for calls with other phones on
                          this router
conference              Adhoc hardware conference configuration
default                 Set a command to its defaults
emergency               Emergency Assistance
exit                    Exit from ephone-template configuration mode
fastdial                Define ip-phone fastdial number
features                define features blocked
group                   set group tag for ephone / ephone-template
keep-conference         Do not disconnect conference when conference
                          initiator hangs-up. Connect remaining parties
                          together directly using call transfer. This command
                          is for adhoc software 3-party conference only.
keepalive               Define keepalive timeout period to unregister IP
```

```
                            phone
keypad-normalize            Normalize keypad messages to 600ms interval
keyphone                    Identify an IP phone as keyphone
max-calls-per-button        Define maximum number of calls per octo-line button
                            of this ephone
mlpp                        Enable Multi-Level Preemption
mtp                         Always send media packets to this router
multicast-moh               Enable Multicast Moh
network-locale              Select the network locale for this template.
night-service               Define night-service bell
no                          Negate a command or set its defaults
nte-end-digit-delay         enforce a delay for sending RTP NTE end digit
                            packets
paging-dn                   set audio paging dn group for phone
park                        set the park information for the ephone
privacy                     Prevent others from viewing or barging calls on a
                            shared octo line. If not set, privacy option under
                            telephony-service will be applied.
privacy-button              Set shared octo line privacy button
service                     Service configuration in ephone template
softkeys                    define softkeys per state
speed-dial                  Define ip-phone speed-dial number
ssh                         enable phone ssh session
transfer                    transfer related configuration
transfer-park               customized transfer to park configuration
transfer-pattern            customized transfer-pattern configuration
type                        Define ip-phone type
url                         Define URL's
user-locale                 Select the user locale for this template.


CME_ROUTER(config-ephone-template)#softkeys ?
alerting                    Softkey order for alerting (ring out) state
connected                   Softkey order for connected state
hold                        Softkey order for HOLD state
idle                        Softkey order for IDLE state
remote-in-use               Softkey order for REMOTE-IN-USE state
ringing                     Softkey order for ringing state
seized                      Softkey order for seized state


CME_ROUTER(config-ephone-template)#softkeys idle ?
Cfwdall                     Call forward all
ConfList                    List all participants in conference
Dnd                         Do not Disturb
Gpickup                     Group Call Pick Up
HLog                        HLog
Join                        Join established call to conference
Login                       Login
Mobility                    Mobility SNR
Newcall                     New call
Pickup                      Call Pick Up
Redial                      Redial
RmLstC                      Remove last conference participant


CME_ROUTER(config-ephone-template)#softkeys idle redial dnd
CME_ROUTER(config-ephone-template)#exit

CME_ROUTER(config)#ephone 12
CME_ROUTER(config-ephone)#ephone-template 6
CME_ROUTER(config-ephone)#restart
CME_ROUTER(config-ephone)#exit
CME_ROUTER(config)#exit
```

❖ Time and date

The time and date format displayed on the IP phones can be modified with the *date-format* and *time-format* commands. The figure 11 shows the outcome of the following example. [22]

CME_ROUTER config (ch4c12):

```
CME_ROUTER#configure terminal
CME_ROUTER(config)#telephony-service
CME_ROUTER(config-telephony)#date-format ?
dd-mm-yy   Set date to dd-mm-yy format
mm-dd-yy   Set date to mm-dd-yy format
yy-dd-mm   Set date to yy-dd-mm format
yy-mm-dd   Set date to yy-mm-dd format
CME_ROUTER(config-telephony)#date-format mm-dd-yy
CME_ROUTER(config-telephony)#time-format ?
12   Set time to 12Hrs(AM/PM) format
24   Set time to 24Hrs format
CME_ROUTER(config-telephony)#time-format 24
CME_ROUTER(config-telephony)#restart all
CME_ROUTER(config-telephony)#exit
CME_ROUTER(config)#exit
```

❖ Description, name and label

To display a custom text description in the header bar of all supported IP phones, we use the *description* command in ephone-dn or ephone-dn-template configuration mode. To return to the default state, we use the *no form* of this command. We use the *name* command to associate a name with a directory number. To remove a name from an extension, we use the *no form* of this command. The label is a text identifier which replaces a phone-number display for an extension on an IP phone console. We use the *label* command in ephone-dn configuration mode. To delete a label, we use the *no form* of this command. The following example and the figure 11 show the modification of all three parameters. [23]

CME_ROUTER config (ch4c13):

```
CME_ROUTER#configure terminal
CME_ROUTER(config)#ephone-dn 11
CME_ROUTER(config-ephone-dn)#description Support
CME_ROUTER(config-ephone-dn)#name Support1
CME_ROUTER(config-ephone-dn)#label Line1
CME_ROUTER(config-ephone-dn)#exit

CME_ROUTER(config)#ephone-dn 12
CME_ROUTER(config-ephone-dn)#description Support
CME_ROUTER(config-ephone-dn)#name Support2
CME_ROUTER(config-ephone-dn)#exit
```

```
CME_ROUTER(config)#ephone-dn 21
CME_ROUTER(config-ephone-dn)#description Customer
CME_ROUTER(config-ephone-dn)#name Customer1
CME_ROUTER(config-ephone-dn)#exit

CME_ROUTER(config)#ephone-dn 22
CME_ROUTER(config-ephone-dn)#description Customer
CME_ROUTER(config-ephone-dn)#name Customer2
CME_ROUTER(config-ephone-dn)#exit

CME_ROUTER(config)#ephone-dn 23
CME_ROUTER(config-ephone-dn)#description Customer
CME_ROUTER(config-ephone-dn)#name Customer3
CME_ROUTER(config-ephone-dn)#exit


CME_ROUTER(config)#telephony-service
CME_ROUTER(config-telephony)#restart all
CME_ROUTER(config-telephony)#exit
CME_ROUTER(config)#exit
```

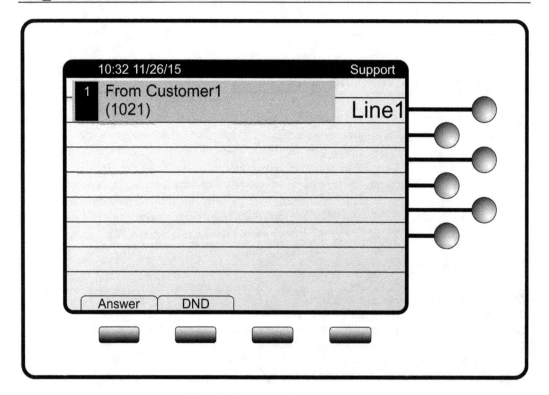

Figure 11: Description, name and label

❖ System message

The system message is a text message displayed on IP phones which are on idle state. Not all the IP phones show the system message. We can use the *system message* command in telephony-service configuration mode. To return to the default, use the *no form* of this command. The following example modifies the system message and the figure 12 shows the result. [23]

CME_ROUTER config (ch4c14):

```
CME_ROUTER#configure terminal
CME_ROUTER(config)#telephony-service
CME_ROUTER(config-telephony)#system message VoIP Lab
CME_ROUTER(config-telephony)#restart all
CME_ROUTER(config-telephony)#exit
CME_ROUTER(config)#exit
```

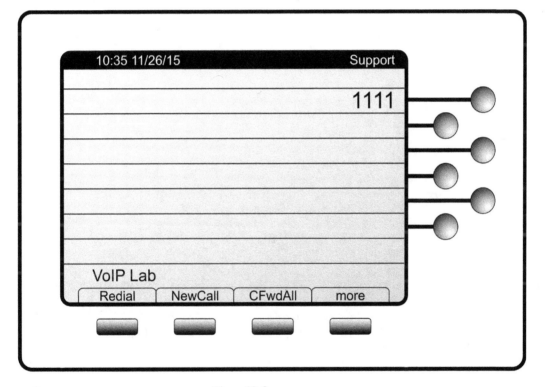

Figure 12: System message

❖ Further study

Further study of the following subjects is advised.

- ephone-template
- softkeys

❖ Quiz

1. Which device can you use to modify CUCME system message?

   A. CUCME Router
   B. Switch
   C. IP phone
   D. CLI

   Answer: A

2. Which of the following commands will change the header bar message of the IP phone to "VoIP"?

   A. name VoIP
   B. description VoIP
   C. header VOIP
   D. telephony-service VoIP header

   Answer: B

3. How many ephone-dn templates can be associated with a single ephone?

   A. None
   B. One
   C. At least one
   D. It is limited by the version of CUCME.

   Answer: B

4. What is the limitation of the "x" button overlay separator?

   A. Single ephone only
   B. Max 6 buttons
   C. No limitations
   D. Cannot be combined with the "c" separator

   Answer: D

5. Which preference value has the highest ephone-dn priority?

   A. 1024
   B. 0
   C. master
   D. 1

   Answer: B

"Intentionally blank"

ADVANCED CONFIGURATION SCCP

CHAPTER 5

Chapter 5: ADVANCED CONFIGURATION SCCP

In this chapter we progress further with the SCCP configuration. We present advanced options and expand caller's opportunities to handle the call in more sophisticated way.

- ❖ Initial configuration
- ❖ Local directory
- ❖ Call forwarding
- ❖ Call transfer
- ❖ Call pickup
- ❖ Call parking
- ❖ Intercom
- ❖ Paging
- ❖ Call blocking
- ❖ Music On Hold
- ❖ Further study
- ❖ Quiz

❖ Initial configuration

The initial topology and configuration of the network for this chapter stays the same as in previous chapters. We setup two ephone-dns and ephones. We will add few more of them later. *Device-security-mode none* command turns off the authentication or encryption between devices to prevent other configuration difficulties. You should use your IP phone *type* in configuration.

CME_ROUTER config (ch5c1):

```
CME_ROUTER#configure terminal
CME_ROUTER(config)#no telephony-service

CME_ROUTER(config)#telephony-service
CME_ROUTER(config-telephony)#ip source-address 172.16.1.1 port
2000
CME_ROUTER(config-telephony)#max-ephones 10
CME_ROUTER(config-telephony)#max-dn 30
CME_ROUTER(config-telephony)#exit

CME_ROUTER(config)#ephone-dn 1 dual-line
CME_ROUTER(config-ephone-dn)#number 1001
CME_ROUTER(config-ephone-dn)#name John Doe
CME_ROUTER(config-ephone-dn)#exit
CME_ROUTER(config)#ephone-dn 2 dual-line
CME_ROUTER(config-ephone-dn)#number 1002
CME_ROUTER(config-ephone-dn)#name Jane Doe
CME_ROUTER(config-ephone-dn)#exit

CME_ROUTER(config)#ephone 1
CME_ROUTER(config-ephone)#mac-address 10BD.0000.0001
CME_ROUTER(config-ephone)#button 1:1
CME_ROUTER(config-ephone)#device-security-mode none
CME_ROUTER(config-ephone)#type 7942
CME_ROUTER(config-ephone)#exit
CME_ROUTER(config)#ephone 2
CME_ROUTER(config-ephone)#mac-address 10BD.0000.0002
CME_ROUTER(config-ephone)#button 1:2
CME_ROUTER(config-ephone)#device-security-mode none
CME_ROUTER(config-ephone)#type 7942
CME_ROUTER(config-ephone)#exit

CME_ROUTER(config)#telephony-service
CME_ROUTER(config-telephony)#reset all
CME_ROUTER(config)#exit
```

❖ Local directory

A local directory is automatically created by CUCME and contains the numbers assigned to ephone-dns. The local directory is accessible for each registered IP phone. Manual directory entries are also allowed. The following configuration enables http server on CME_ROUTER. It is a necessary step to allow IP phones to access Local directory folder. The URL of Local directory must be specified (http://172.16.1.1/localdirectory). A directory order can be also specified. The example configures a manual directory entry for the number 9999. Configuration files have to be updated to apply changes in the Local directory. [24]

CME_ROUTER config (ch5c2):

```
CME_ROUTER#configure terminal
CME_ROUTER(config)#ip http server

CME_ROUTER(config)#telephony-service
CME_ROUTER(config-telephony)#url directories
http://172.16.1.1/localdirectory
CME_ROUTER(config-telephony)#service local-directory
CME_ROUTER(config-telephony)#directory last-name-first

CME_ROUTER(config-telephony)#directory entry 1 9999 name Jimmy
Chairon

CME_ROUTER(config-telephony)#create cnf-files

CME_ROUTER(config-telephony)#reset all
CME_ROUTER(config-telephony)#exit
CME_ROUTER(config)#exit
```

The local directory can be browsed by an IP phone user in the following way.

- Press *Directories* softkey on the IP phone.
- Select *Local directory*.
- Type the *First* or *Last* name. In case we leave the fields blank, all users in local directory will be displayed.

❖ Call forwarding

In case we want to answer the call on the IP phone which is located elsewhere, we can use call forwarding feature to direct the call from one IP phone to another. There are basically two types of forwarding available. The first one is user based dynamic call forwarding. The second one is a static and can be configured directly on CUCME.

We need to add another IP phone to the existing configuration.

CME_ROUTER config (ch5c3):

```
CME_ROUTER#configure terminal
CME_ROUTER(config)#ephone-dn 3 dual-line
CME_ROUTER(config-ephone-dn)#number 1003
CME_ROUTER(config-ephone-dn)#name Frank Tableton
CME_ROUTER(config-ephone-dn)#exit

CME_ROUTER(config)#ephone 3
CME_ROUTER(config-ephone)#mac-address 10BD.0000.0003
CME_ROUTER(config-ephone)#button 1:3
CME_ROUTER(config-ephone)#device-security-mode none
CME_ROUTER(config-ephone)#type 7942
CME_ROUTER(config-ephone)#restart
CME_ROUTER(config-ephone)#exit
CME_ROUTER(config)#exit
```

Dynamic call forwarding

We press *CFwdAll* softkey on the IP phone associated with the number 1003 (ephone 3). The IP phone is waiting for a new number, to which all the calls will be forwarded. After we enter 1002, we press the *EndCall* softkey. A home screen is displayed immediately with the "Forwarded to 1002" message. Now, if we dial 1003 from ephone 1, the call is automatically forwarded to the ephone 2. We can cancel the call forwarding by pressing the *CFwdAll* softkey on ephone 3 and the message "Forwarded to 1002" disappears.

Static call forwarding

Static call forwarding has more options than its dynamic version. Static forwarding can be overridden, using the dynamic call forwarding. Static forwarding has multiple options. [25]

```
CME_ROUTER#configure terminal
CME_ROUTER(config)#ephone-dn 1
CME_ROUTER(config-ephone-dn)#call-forward ?
all           forward all calls
busy          forward call on busy
max-length    max number of digits allowed for CFwdAll from IP phone
night-service forward call on activated night-service
noan          forward call on no-answer
CME_ROUTER(config-ephone-dn)#call-forward noan 1003 timeout ?
< 3-60000 > Ringing no answer timeout duration in seconds
CME_ROUTER(config-ephone-dn)#call-forward noan 1003 timeout 10
CME_ROUTER(config-ephone-dn)#exit
CME_ROUTER(config)#exit
```

If we call 1001 from the ephone 2 and do not answer, the call will be forwarded to ephone 3 after 10 seconds.

❖ Call transfer

Call transfer moves the active call from one number to another. On the IP phone, we perform this task by pressing the *Trnsfer* softkey and dialing the number, to which we want to forward the call. The call is immediately forwarded. We can configure different forwarding modes for ephone-dns.

CME_ROUTER config (ch5c4):

```
CME_ROUTER#configure terminal
CME_ROUTER(config)#ephone-dn 1
CME_ROUTER(config-ephone-dn)#transfer-mode ?
blind Perform blind call transfers (without consultation) using single
phone line
consult Perform call transfers with consultation using second phone line if
available
CME_ROUTER(config-ephone-dn)#transfer-mode blind
CME_ROUTER(config-ephone-dn)#exit

CME_ROUTER(config)#ephone-dn 2
CME_ROUTER(config-ephone-dn)#transfer-mode consult
CME_ROUTER(config-ephone-dn)#exit
CME_ROUTER(config)#exit
```

Blind mode

If we call 1001 from the ephone 3 and transfer the call using *Trnsfer* softkey on the ephone 1 to the number 1002, the call will be transferred immediately and the ephone 3 and the ephone 2 are in active call.

Consult mode

We call 1002 from the ephone 3 and transfer the call using *Trnsfer* softkey on the ephone 2 to the number 1001. Initially, the ephone 2 and the ephone 1 are in active consult call. Right after the ephone 2 terminates the call with the ephone 1, the ephone 1 and the ephone 3 are in active call. [25]

❖ Call pickup

We can use existing configuration to test Call pickup. Call pickup allows a user to answer the remote extension on the local IP phone. *PickUp* softkey does the trick. We dial 1003 from the ephone 1 to reach the ephone 3. While the ephone 3 is ringing, we press the Pickup softkey on the ephone 2 and enter the number 1003. The call is immediately picked and the ephone 3 stops ringing.

❖ Call parking

Call parking allows us to park an active call. It has a similar functionality as hold, except it is possible to resume the call from any IP phone. An additional ephone-dn has to be configured. It will serve as parking slot and will not be assigned to any button. [26]

CME_ROUTER config (ch5c5):

```
CME_ROUTER#configure terminal
CME_ROUTER(config)#ephone-dn 11
CME_ROUTER(config-ephone-dn)#number 1111
CME_ROUTER(config-ephone-dn)#name Parking
CME_ROUTER(config-ephone-dn)#park-slot
CME_ROUTER(config-ephone-dn)#exit
CME_ROUTER(config)#exit
```

To test the Call parking we dial 1003 from the ephone 1 to reach the ephone 3. We answer the call. With the call still active we use *Transfer* softkey on the ephone 3 to transfer the call from 1003 to 1111. After entering the 1111, the call is parked. We can pick up the call from the ephone 2 by pressing the *PickUp* softkey and entering the number 1111.

❖ Intercom

The intercom is basically a speed dial with an automatic answer on a loudspeaker. A microphone is muted by default. We setup two new ephone-dns for an intercom between two IP phones. We can use A, B or C letters as a part of the number to avoid accidental dialing. We assign ephone-dn 15 to the second button of the ephone 1 and ephone-dn 16 to the second button of the ephone 2. There are few different options how intercom may behave. Let us consider a "BOSS-WORKER" scenario. The boss will dial the worker intercom and the worker extension is automatically answered with an unmuted speaker. On the other hand, the worker can dial the boss intercom, but the worker must wait till the boss answers the call. In this scenario the ephone 1 belongs to the boss and the ephone 2 to the worker. If the boss presses the "WORKER" button on the ephone 1, the intercom is automatically answered and unmuted on the ephone 2. If the worker presses the "BOSS" button on the ephone 2, the intercom rings on the ephone 1 and the call has to be answered by the boss to be active. [27]

CME_ROUTER config (ch5c6):

```
CME_ROUTER#configure terminal
CME_ROUTER(config)# ephone-dn 15
CME_ROUTER(config-ephone-dn)# number A15
CME_ROUTER(config-ephone-dn)#intercom A16 no-auto-answer label
"Worker"
CME_ROUTER(config-ephone-dn)# exit
CME_ROUTER(config)# ephone-dn 16
CME_ROUTER(config-ephone-dn)# number A16
CME_ROUTER(config-ephone-dn)#intercom A15 no-mute label "Boss"
```

```
CME_ROUTER(config-ephone-dn)# exit
CME_ROUTER(config)# ephone 1
CME_ROUTER(config-ephone)# button 2:15
CME_ROUTER(config-ephone)# restart
CME_ROUTER(config-ephone)# exit
CME_ROUTER(config)# ephone 2
CME_ROUTER(config-ephone)# button 2:16
CME_ROUTER(config-ephone)# restart
CME_ROUTER(config-ephone)#exit
CME_ROUTER(config)#exit
```

❖ Paging

Paging represents a one way intercom. Paging is usually broadcast across multiple IP phones. Paging can be configured as a unicast or a broadcast. The unicast paging generates a great amount of overhead in the network. The multicast, on the other hand, is more efficient. Addresses in the range of 224.0.0.0 to 293.255.255.255 are considered multicast addresses. They can be used for paging, except for 244.X.X.X range. [28]

CME_ROUTER config (ch5c7):

```
CME_ROUTER#configure terminal
CME_ROUTER(config)#ephone-dn 17
CME_ROUTER(config-ephone-dn)#number 9999
CME_ROUTER(config-ephone-dn)#paging ip 239.15.1.25 port 2000
CME_ROUTER(config-ephone-dn)#exit

CME_ROUTER(config)#ephone 1
CME_ROUTER(config-ephone)#paging-dn 17 multicast
CME_ROUTER(config-ephone)#exit
CME_ROUTER(config)#ephone 2
CME_ROUTER(config-ephone)#paging-dn 17 multicast
CME_ROUTER(config-ephone)#exit
CME_ROUTER(config)#exit
```

If we dial the number 9999 from the ephone 3, ephones 1 and 2 will answer automatically with the loudspeaker unmuted. Users on the booth ephones can listen to the call from the ephone 3, but cannot respond.

❖ Call blocking

There are multiple ways how to prevent users from making calls. Several restrictions can be applied to limit the access for specific users. Not everyone should be allowed to dial long distance calls or use the IP phone after working hours. We can use *after-hours* command for call blocking based on time and a dialing number. The following example shows how to block the calls based on a specific time, date and set of numbers. We use the actual date and time to test the scenario.

CME_ROUTER config (ch5c8):

```
CME_ROUTER#show clock
*11:09:23.055 UTC Mon Feb 1 2016
CME_ROUTER(config)#telephony-service
CME_ROUTER(config-telephony)#after-hours day Mon 10:00 23:59
CME_ROUTER(config-telephony)#after-hours date Feb 29 00:00 23:59
CME_ROUTER(config-telephony)#after-hours block pattern 1 10..
CME_ROUTER(config-telephony)#exit
CME_ROUTER(config)#exit
```

Now, if we dial any number starting with 10 followed by two digits, we get the busy signal. It is possible to define an override code which can be used to revoke blocking any IP phone. The global override code is configured as follows.

```
CME_ROUTER#confure terminal
CME_ROUTER(config)#telephony-service
CME_ROUTER(config-telephony)# after-hours override-code 0303
CME_ROUTER(config-telephony)#exit
CME_ROUTER(config)#exit
```

If we dial 0303 on the ephone 3 and immediately enter the arbitrary active number, for example 1001, the ephone 1 will ring and we can answer the call from the ephone 3. Dial blocking is disabled only for the IP phone on which we entered the global override code. It is not possible to make the call from another IP phone without entering the code. Pin code (different code) follows the same concept but it is defined on the IP phone. Each ephone can have a different pin code. In the following example we assign the 0606 pin code to the ephone 1. To make the pin login active on the IP phones, we need to use *login* command in telephony-service. The *timeout* parameter defines the interval after which the login session is destroyed. The c*lear* parameter destroys all the login sessions at 23:00 and users need to log in again. [29]

```
CME_ROUTER#confure terminal
CME_ROUTER(config)#ephone 1
CME_ROUTER(config-ephone)# pin 0606
CME_ROUTER(config-ephone)# exit

CME_ROUTER(config)#telephony-service
CME_ROUTER(config-telephony)#login timeout 120 clear 23:00
CME_ROUTER(config-telephony)#restart all
CME_ROUTER(config-telephony)#exit
CME_ROUTER(config)#exit
```

```
CME_ROUTER# sh ephone login
ephone 1        Pin enabled:TRUE        Logged-in:FALSE
ephone 2        Pin enabled:FALSE
ephone 3        Pin enabled:FALSE
```

We can check the active status of pin assignments and active login sessions by entering the command *sh ephone login*. We can see that the ephone 1 has its pin enabled but the user is not logged yet. We can log in using the *Login* softkey on the IP phone. By default the Login softkey is dimmed and not accessible. We can enable it by entering the *login* command in telephony-service, which we already did.

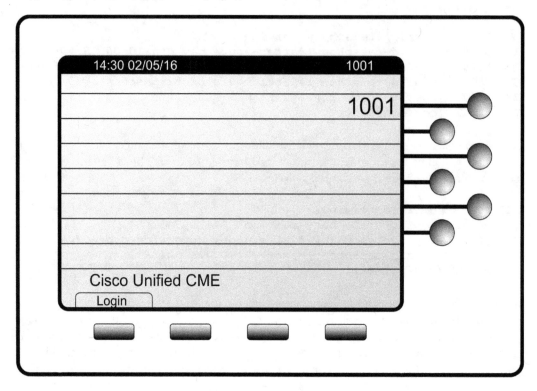

Figure 13: IP phone pin login

After we press the *Login* softkey and enter the pin 0606 on the ephone 1, we can make calls without any restrictions. We can test it by dialing 1002 from the ephone 1. The ephone 2 is ringing and we can answer the call. We can also check the status by entering the *sh ephone login* command again.

```
CME_ROUTER# sh ephone login
ephone 1        Pin enabled:TRUE        Logged-in:TRUE
ephone 2        Pin enabled:FALSE
ephone 3        Pin enabled:FALSE
```

We can also completely exempt the IP phone from the blocking. In the following example we exempt the ephone 2 from the blocking. We can test the configuration by dialing 1001 from the ephone 2.

```
CME_ROUTER#confure terminal
CME_ROUTER(config)#ephone 2
CME_ROUTER(config-ephone)# after-hour exempt
CME_ROUTER(config-telephony)#exit
CME_ROUTER(config)#exit
```

We can also block selected numbers 24-7. We can test this by blocking the paging number 9999 which we configured for the paging in this chapter.

```
Router#confure terminal
Router(config)#telephony-service
Router(config-telephony)#after-hours block pattern 3 9999 7-24
CME_ROUTER(config-telephony)#exit
CME_ROUTER(config)#exit
```

If we call the number 9999 from any ephone, we get the busy tone 24-7. All the blocking restrictions can be canceled by entering the *no* form of *after-hours* command.

❖ Music On Hold

Music on hold plays the selected music file while a caller is on hold. It makes waiting less painful and users know that they are waiting for a call and have not been disconnected. Music files have to be stored on the router flash and they have to follow some rules to be successfully played during the hold. We can copy music files to the router flash using the TFTP server, (the process of copying files over TFTP was already presented) or we can use CompactFlash card reader to copy music files to the flash. The list of files included on the flash can be displayed using the *show flash:* command. As we can see our flash has music-on-hold.au file on it. Compatible music files must meet following requirements:

- au or wav file format
- G.711 codec
- 8-bit rate at 8kHz
- be careful with the copyrighted music [30]

CME_ROUTER config (ch5c9):

```
CME_ROUTER#show flash:
*Feb  8 12:04:09.663: %SYS-5-CONFIG_I: Configured from console by console
-#- --length-- -----date/time------ path
Omitted output
10      496521 Feb 08 2016 00:52:18 music-on-hold.au
```

Music on hold can be distributed as a unicast or a multicast stream. A unicast music on hold is configured if the *multicast* command is not included. Unicast streaming consumes a notable amount of bandwidth. Multicast is a more efficient solution. However, it is not usable in the scenarios with multiple subnets. In that case, unicast is the only choice. We apply the same rules for the range of usable multicast addresses as for previously mentioned paging.

```
CME_ROUTER#confure terminal
CME_ROUTER(config)#telephony-service
CME_ROUTER(config-telephony)#moh music-on-hold.au
CME_ROUTER(config-telephony)# multicast moh 239.25.5.15 port 2000
CME_ROUTER(config-telephony)#restart all
CME_ROUTER(config-telephony)#exit
CME_ROUTER(config)#exit
```

We can test the configuration by dialing 1001 from the ephone 2. We answer the call on the ephone 1 and put it on hold. Music on hold should play on the ephone 2.

❖ Further study

CUCME contains far more advanced services and functions. If the set presented in this chapter does not contain service or function you are looking for, further study is advised.

❖ Quiz

1. Which audio format is compatible with the music on hold?

   A. gif
   B. wav
   C. uc
   D. mp3

   Answer: B

2. The *CFwdAll* softkey is used for

   A. Dynamic call forwarding
   B. Static call forwarding
   C. Call pickup
   D. Call fast forward

   Answer: A

3. Which one of the following modes can be configured for the call transfer?

   A. Direct
   B. Personal
   C. Blind
   D. Custom

   Answer: C

4. What does the proper function of the call parking require?

   A. Ephone-dn park-slot
   B. Call timeout
   C. Parking softkey
   D. Parking IP address

   Answer: A

5. Which one of the following options is similar to the intercom?

   A. Call pickup
   B. Local directory
   C. Paging
   D. Call transfer
   E. Remote access

   Answer: C

"Intentionally blank"

PSTN VOICE GATEWAY SCCP

CHAPTER 6

Chapter 6: PSTN VOICE GATEWAY SCCP

Local VoIP network usually connects to the larger aggregation of networks called The Public Switched Telephone Network (PSTN). The following chapter presents the configuration of CME_ROUTER and Private Branch Exchange (PBX) interconnection, which allows us to make the call beyond the local network. This chapter requires an access to a real or an emulated PBX connection. In this chapter we also present the integration of an analog telephone with a dial pad or a rotary dial into the VoIP network.

- ❖ Network topology scheme
- ❖ Hardware requirements
- ❖ FXS Analog phone configuration
- ❖ FXO PBX
- ❖ Further study
- ❖ Quiz

❖ Network topology scheme

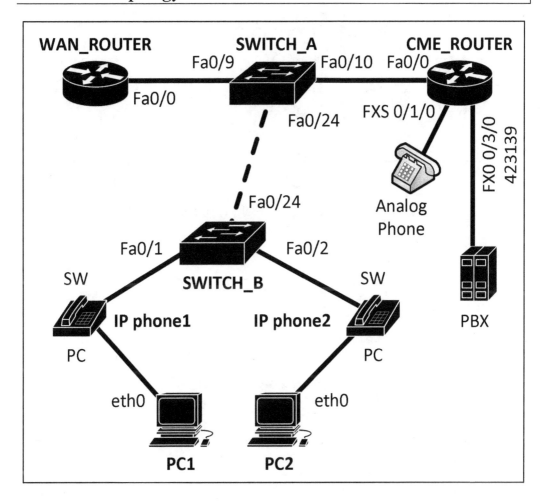

Figure 14: Network topology scheme

❖ Hardware requirements

Compared with previous chapters, topology is slightly different. We need to use a router with a special set of ports which allow us to connect an analog phone and a PBX. The router also has to include Digital Signal Processing (DSP) module in order to process voice and signaling features. Foreign Exchange Station (FXS) and Foreign Exchange Office (FXO) interface modules are required to accomplish the task.

Figure 15: FXS and FXO modules

The initial configuration requires setting up basic telephony parameters, two dual line ephone-dns and two ephones.

CME_ROUTER config (ch6c1):

```
CME_ROUTER#configure terminal
CME_ROUTER(config)#no telephony-service

CME_ROUTER(config)#telephony-service
CME_ROUTER(config-telephony)#ip source-address 172.16.1.1 port
2000
CME_ROUTER(config-telephony)#max-ephones 10
CME_ROUTER(config-telephony)#max-dn 30
CME_ROUTER(config-telephony)#exit
CME_ROUTER(config)#exit
CME_ROUTER(config)#ephone-dn 1 dual-line
CME_ROUTER(config-ephone-dn)#number 1001
CME_ROUTER(config-ephone-dn)#name IP1
CME_ROUTER(config-ephone-dn)#exit
CME_ROUTER(config)#ephone-dn 2 dual-line
CME_ROUTER(config-ephone-dn)#number 1002
CME_ROUTER(config-ephone-dn)#name IP2
CME_ROUTER(config-ephone-dn)#exit
CME_ROUTER(config)#ephone 1
CME_ROUTER(config-ephone)#mac-address 10BD.0000.0001
CME_ROUTER(config-ephone)#button 1:1
CME_ROUTER(config-ephone)#device-security-mode none
CME_ROUTER(config-ephone)#type 7942
CME_ROUTER(config-ephone)#restart
CME_ROUTER(config-ephone)#exit
CME_ROUTER(config)#ephone 2
CME_ROUTER(config-ephone)#mac-address 10BD.0000.0002
CME_ROUTER(config-ephone)#button 1:2
CME_ROUTER(config-ephone)#device-security-mode none
CME_ROUTER(config-ephone)#type 7942
CME_ROUTER(config-ephone)#restart
CME_ROUTER(config-ephone)#exit
CME_ROUTER(config)#exit
```

❖ FXS Analog phone configuration

FXS analog voice card is detected and added as a new voice interface to the router configuration. We can check it by displaying a running configuration. FXS ports are responsible for connecting analog endpoint devices such as analog phones, fax machines, and modems. Our next example will explain the configuration of an analog phone.

Figure 16: Analog phone

CME_ROUTER config (ch6c2):

```
CME_ROUTER#show running-config | begin voice-port
voice-port 0/1/0
!
voice-port 0/1/1
!
voice-port 0/3/0
!
voice-port 0/3/1
```

```
CME_ROUTER#show voice port summary
                                         IN        OUT
PORT             CH  SIG-TYPE   ADMIN OPER STATUS   STATUS    EC
=============== == ============= ===== ==== ======== ======== ==
0/1/0            -- fxs-ls       up    dorm on-hook  idle      y
0/1/1            -- fxs-ls       up    dorm on-hook  idle      y
0/3/0            -- fxo-ls       up    dorm idle     on-hook   y
0/3/1            -- fxo-ls       up    dorm idle     on-hook   y
```

We configure the number 1010 for the analog phone on FXS voice port 0/1/0. The analog phone has to be connected to the correct port using RJ12 connector to function properly. Firstly, we need to enable *caller-id* because it is disabled by default. Analog phone is not a smart device, it has no idea which number is assigned to it. However, it is easier to swap analog phones without worrying about the firmware or configuration issues. *Station-id* command helps us to configure the number and the name for the FXS port 0/1/0. [31]

```
CME_ROUTER#configure terminal
CME_ROUTER(config)#voice-port 0/1/0
CME_ROUTER(config-voiceport)#caller-id enable
CME_ROUTER(config-voiceport)#station-id number 1010
CME_ROUTER(config-voiceport)#station-id name Analog Phone
```

Location options can be set up by using the command *cptone*.

```
CME_ROUTER(config-voiceport)#cptone ?
AR Argentina          IN India            PA Panama
AU Australia          ID Indonesia        PE Peru
AT Austria            IE Ireland          PH Philippines
.
. Omitted output
.
FI Finland            NP Nepal            TH Thailand
FR France             NL Netherlands      TR Turkey
DE Germany            NZ New Zealand      AE United Arab Emirates
GH Ghana              NG Nigeria          GB United Kingdom
GR Greece             NO Norway           US United States
HK Hong Kong          OM Oman             VE Venezuela
HU Hungary            PK Pakistan         ZW Zimbabwe
IS Iceland

CME_ROUTER(config-voiceport)#cptone US
```

Analog telephones may be country dependent. Ringing frequency needs to be modified according of the location to ring properly. Frequencies are measured in Hertz.

```
CME_ROUTER(config-voiceport)#ring frequency ?
20  ring frequency 20 Hertz
25  ring frequency 25 Hertz
30  ring frequency 30 Hertz
50  ring frequency 50 Hertz

CME_ROUTER(config-voiceport)#ring frequency 50
CME_ROUTER(config-voiceport)#exit
CME_ROUTER(config)#exit
```

We can check in depth voice port parameters.

```
CME_ROUTER# show voice port 0/1/0
Foreign Exchange Station 0/1/0 Slot is 0, Sub-unit is 1, Port is 0
 Type of VoicePort is FXS  VIC3-2FXS/DID
 Operation State is DORMANT
 Administrative State is UP
 No Interface Down Failure
 Description is not set
 Noise Regeneration is enabled
 Non Linear Processing is enabled
 Non Linear Mute is disabled
 Non Linear Threshold is -21 dB
 Music On Hold Threshold is Set to -38 dBm
 In Gain is Set to 0 dB
 Out Attenuation is Set to 3 dB
 Echo Cancellation is enabled
 Echo Cancellation NLP mute is disabled
 Echo Cancellation NLP threshold is -21 dB
 Echo Cancel Coverage is set to 128 ms
 Echo Cancel worst case ERL is set to 6 dB
 Playout-delay Mode is set to adaptive
 Playout-delay Nominal is set to 60 ms
 Playout-delay Maximum is set to 1000 ms
 Playout-delay Minimum mode is set to default, value 40 ms
 Playout-delay Fax is set to 300 ms
 Connection Mode is normal
 Connection Number is not set
 Initial Time Out is set to 15 s
 Interdigit Time Out is set to 10 s
 Call Disconnect Time Out is set to 60 s
 Supervisory Disconnect Time Out is set to 750 ms
 Ringing Time Out is set to 180 s
 Wait Release Time Out is set to 30 s
 Companding Type is u-law
 Region Tone is set for SK

 Analog Info Follows:
 Currently processing none
 Maintenance Mode Set to None (not in mtc mode)
 Number of signaling protocol errors are 0
 Impedance is set to 600r Ohm
 Station name Analog Phone, Station number 1010

 Caller ID Info Follows:
 Standard BELLCORE
 Output attenuation is set to 14 dB
 Caller ID is transmitted after 1 ring(s)
 Translation profile (Incoming):
 Translation profile (Outgoing):
 lpcor (Incoming):
 lpcor (Outgoing):

 Voice card specific Info Follows:
 Signal Type is loopStart
 Ring Frequency is 50 Hz
 Hook Status is On Hook
 Ring Active Status is inactive
 Ring Ground Status is inactive
 Tip Ground Status is inactive
 Digit Duration Timing is set to 100 ms
 InterDigit Duration Timing is set to 100 ms
 Hookflash-in Timing is set to max=1000 ms, min=150 ms
 Hookflash-out Timing is set to 400 ms
 No disconnect acknowledge
 Ring Cadence is defined by CPTone Selection
```

```
Ring Cadence are [10 40] * 100 msec
Ringer Equivalence Number is set to 1
```

Finally, we need to specify a destination port for 1010 calls using *dial-peer*.

```
CME_ROUTER#configure terminal
CME_ROUTER(config)#dial-peer voice ?
< 1-2147483647 > Voice dial-peer tag

CME_ROUTER(config)#dial-peer voice 1010 pots
CME_ROUTER(config-dial-peer)#destination-pattern 1010
CME_ROUTER(config-dial-peer)#port 0/1/0
CME_ROUTER(config-dial-peer)#exit
CME_ROUTER(config)#exit
```

We can test the configuration by calling the number 1001 from the Analog Phone. And we can also try to call the number 1010 from the ephone 1. Both calls should be successful.

❖ FXO PBX

FXO allows us to interconnect the existing VoIP topology with the PBX. FXO configuration is very similar to the previous FXS configuration. We specify the name and number using *station-id* command. The number is assigned by the PBX administrator. Using the *signal groundStart* we enable a ground signaling method for PSTN.

CME_ROUTER config (ch6c3):

```
CME_ROUTER#configure terminal
CME_ROUTER(config)#voice-port 0/3/0
CME_ROUTER(config-voiceport)#station-id name PBX
CME_ROUTER(config-voiceport)#station-id number 423139
CME_ROUTER(config-voiceport)#signal groundStart
```

Unlike the FXS configuration we also need to configure a dial-type. Dial pad phones usually use the Dual Tone Multi Frequency (DTMF) and rotary dial phones usually use the pulse.

```
CME_ROUTER(config-voiceport)#dial-type dtmf
```

The ring-number command specifies that the FXO does not answer the call until after the second ring.

```
CME_ROUTER(config-voiceport)#ring number 2
CME_ROUTER(config-voiceport)#exit
```

We need to configure *dial-peer* to route the calls to the specific port.

```
CME_ROUTER#configure terminal
CME_ROUTER(config)#dial-peer voice 420000 pots
CME_ROUTER(config-dial-peer)#destination-pattern 42....
CME_ROUTER(config-dial-peer)#no digit-strip
CME_ROUTER(config-dial-peer)#port 0/3/0
CME_ROUTER(config-dial-peer)#exit
CME_ROUTER(config)#exit
```

If any phone dials the 42XXXX number, the calls will be routed over to the legacy PBX on FXO port 0/3/0. In our topology the FXO port connected to the PBX has 423139 number assigned by the PBX administrator. The simplest way how to deliver calls from PSTN to IP phones is to set up a receptionist extension. We use the IP phone 1001, which has been already configured. All we need to do is to configure the FXO port for a proper signaling and set up the Private Line Automatic Ringdown (PLAR) to point to extension 1001. [32]

```
CME_ROUTER#configure-terminal
CME_ROUTER(config)#voice-port 0/3/0
CME_ROUTER(config)#signal groundStart
CME_ROUTER(config-voiceport)#connection plar 1001
CME_ROUTER(config-voiceport)#exit
CME_ROUTER(config)#exit
```

If the receptionist receives the call from PBX, it is possible to answer the call and, if needed, forward it to any IP phone by using a dynamic forwarding. Direct calls from the IP phones to the PBX are possible, as well.

❖ Further study

Further study of the following subjects is advised.

- DTMF and PULSE dialing
- PBX
- Dial peer

❖ Quiz

1. Which expansion card allows us to interconnect PBX with CUCME?

    A. FXS
    B. FXO
    C. PLAR
    D. DTMF

    Answer: B

2. Which of the following options represents FXS ports in router configuration?

    A. Dynamic forwarding
    B. Telephony service
    C. Voice ports
    D. Call ports

    Answer: C

3. Which type of connector does an analog phone use?

    A. RJ12
    B. RJ45
    C. RJ48C
    D. Custom

    Answer: A

4. Is analog phone powered by the local power brick?

    A. Yes
    B. No

    Answer: B

5. Which firmware is required for the analog phone to function properly?

    A. SIP
    B. SCCP
    C. None
    D. At least 14.2

    Answer: C

"Intentionally blank"

IP PHONES SIP

CHAPTER 7

Functional topology and the configuration presented in the chapter two is the starting point for this chapter. The chapter summarizes the process of basic configuration of CUCME together with the IP phone registration procedure and the IP phone SIP firmware selection and upload. In this chapter an IP Communicator is configured so that it can be used with the SIP.

- ❖ Basic CUCME SIP configuration

- ❖ IP Communicator

- ❖ Further study

- ❖ Show running-config

- ❖ Quiz

❖ Basic CUCME SIP configuration

An IP phone may correctly operate right after it is connected and successfully registered. This means that the IP phone firmware has been already downloaded by the IP phone. If we perform factory reset or the IP phone does not have the firmware loaded for some reason, it will display MAC address and the message "Upgrading". In that case, the IP phone tries to download appropriate firmware files from the TFTP server. If the files are included on the TFTP server, the IP phone will download and install them. If not, we need to upload them to the server and register them. The following example illustrates how to upload and register the IP phone firmware files. Firstly, we need to download appropriate files for SIP. Search the IP phone vendor site for the firmware files. The firmware files usually come in compressed form like tar files. A compressed file includes multiple firmware files for an IP phone. There is no need to decompress the file on your PC after the download. We will use the TFTP to upload it to the CME_ROUTER and decompress it on the place. We will use the PC1 for this purpose. We need to check the IP address of the PC1. It was delivered by the DHCP from WAN_ROUTER from DHCP data pool. One option is to use "ipconfig" in a command line window. The PC1 received IP address 172.16.5.10, your PC could and almost surely received a different IP address, but it has to be from the same DHCP data pool.

```
C:\Users\cisco>ipconfig

Windows IP Configuration

Ethernet adapter Ethernet:

   Connection-specific DNS Suffix  . :
   Link-local IPv6 Address . . . . . : fe80::18b3:3e67:c90:1438%3
   IPv4 Address. . . . . . . . . . . : 172.16.5.10
   Subnet Mask . . . . . . . . . . . : 255.255.255.0
   Default Gateway . . . . . . . . . : 172.16.5.254
```

Figure 17: PC IP configuration

Download and run TFTP software of your choice on the PC1. All we need to do is run the software and choose the directory where the tar firmware file is located. We also need to choose the interface configured with the IP address 172.16.5.10. Now all is set and ready.

99

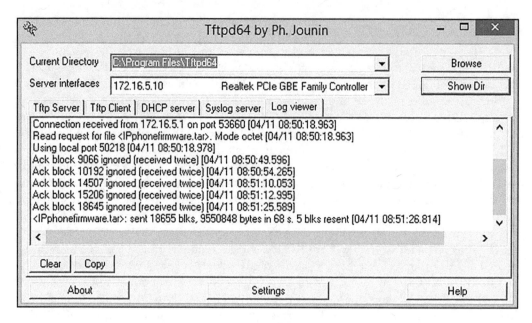

Figure 18: PC TFTP server

We will use CME_ROUTER to download files from TFTP server that we setup on the PC1. We need to check if PC1 is reachable from CME_ROUTER for a successful download. We will use the *ping* command to accomplish that.

CME_ROUTER config (ch7c1):

```
CME_ROUTER#ping 172.16.5.10
Type escape sequence to abort.
Sending 5, 100-byte ICMP Echos to 172.16.5.10, timeout is 2 seconds:
.!!!!
Success rate is 100 percent (5/5), round-trip min/avg/max = 1/1/1 ms
```

PC1 is fully reachable and a download is possible. The following command downloads tar file from the PC1 and decompressed it on the router's flash card. Be careful with the tar file name. It must correspond with the name of SIP firmware file located on the PC1.

```
CME_ROUTER#archive tar /xtract
tftp://172.16.5.10/IPphonefirmware.tar flash:
Loading IPphonefirmware.tar from 172.16.5.10 (via FastEthernet0/0.50): !
extracting apps42.8-4-1-23.sbn (2918613 bytes)!!!!!!!!!!!!
extracting cnu42.8-4-1-23.sbn (485066 bytes)!!
extracting cvm42sip.8-4-1-23.sbn (3047459 bytes)O!!!!!!!!!!!!!
extracting dsp42.8-4-1-23.sbn (335003 bytes)O!
extracting jar42sip.8-4-1-23.sbn (630128 bytes)!!
extracting SIP42.8-4-2S.loads (656 bytes)O
extracting term42.default.loads (660 bytes)
extracting term62.default.loads (660 bytes)!
[OK - 7426048 bytes]
```

After a successful download all the files should be located on CME_ROUTER flash card. We can check it with the *show flash:* command. A flash card contains an IOS file and IP phone firmware files. Your flash card may contain many other files too. We can possibly use other methods to transfer firmware files to the flash card. For example, use the card reader on your PC. Remove the card from the router, insert it to your reader, extract and copy the files directly to the card. Insert it back to the router and we are good to go. However, this approach requires physical access to the router device and may not be the best solution for the enterprise environment. All the downloaded files have to be registered with the TFTP server to be reachable for the IP phone. *Tftp-server* command allows us to register the files. Firmware for different types of IP phones use different file names and the number of files also differ.

```
CME_ROUTER#configure terminal
CME_ROUTER(config)#tftp-server flash:apps42.8-4-1-23.sbn
CME_ROUTER(config)#tftp-server flash:cnu42.8-4-1-23.sbn
CME_ROUTER(config)#tftp-server flash:cvm42sip.8-4-1-23.sbn
CME_ROUTER(config)#tftp-server flash:dsp42.8-4-1-23.sbn
CME_ROUTER(config)#tftp-server flash:jar42sip.8-4-1-23.sbn
CME_ROUTER(config)#tftp-server flash:SIP42.8-4-2S.loads
CME_ROUTER(config)#tftp-server flash:term42.default.loads
CME_ROUTER(config)#tftp-server flash:term62.default.loads
CME_ROUTER(config)#exit
```

Basic IP phones SIP setup requires to active the voice service. At the moment, we present minimal basic configuration to complete the task. We access the *voice service voip* configuration mod and specify that we will use only SIP connections. There are also other possible inter-protocol variants, but they are out of the scope of this book. In the sip configuration mode we specify the intervals for IP phones re-registration.

CME_ROUTER config (ch7c2):

```
CME_ROUTER#configure terminal
CME_ROUTER(config)#voice service voip
CME_ROUTER(conf-voi-serv)#allow-connections sip to sip
CME_ROUTER(conf-voi-serv)#sip
CME_ROUTER(conf-serv-sip)#registrar server expires max 1200 min
300
CME_ROUTER(conf-serv-sip)#exit
CME_ROUTER(conf-voi-serv)#exit
```

After a successful TFTP registration, firmware needs to be associated with the specific type of IP phone. If we use *load* command followed by a question mark, the console displays all the supported types. The group of supported types depends on which of IOS and CUCME is installed on the router. IP phones now should be able to download and install firmware. One specific type of the IP phone needs only one registration of firmware even if we use multiple phones of the same type in our network. If we include multiple types of IP phones, we need to complete registration for each type separately. IP phone vendor download page provides you with convenient information which files you need to register and load in CUCME. This entire configuration is done in *voice register global*. *Max-dn* and *max-pool* commands are not directly related to the firmware registration and they will be explained later.

```
CME_ROUTER(config)#voice register global
CME_ROUTER(config-register-global)#mode cme

CME_ROUTER(config-register-global)#source-address 172.16.1.1 port
5060
CME_ROUTER(config-register-global)#max-dn 30
CME_ROUTER(config-register-global)#max-pool 10
CME_ROUTER(config-register-global)#load ?
  3911        Select the firmware load file for 3911
  3951        Select the firmware load file for 3951
  7905        Select the firmware load file for 7905
  7906        Select the firmware load file for TNP 7906 phone
  7911        Select the firmware load file for TNP 7911 phone
  7912        Select the firmware load file for 7912
  7941        Select the firmware load file for TNP 7941 phones
  7941GE      Select the firmware load file for TNP 7941GE phones
  7942        Select the firmware load file for TNP 7942 phones
  7945        Select the firmware load file for TNP 7945 phones
  7960-7940   Select the firmware load file for Telecaster 7960 & 7940 phones
  7961        Select the firmware load file for TNP 7961 phones
  7961GE      Select the firmware load file for TNP 7961GE phones
  7962        Select the firmware load file for TNP 7962 phones
  7965        Select the firmware load file for TNP 7965 phones
  7970        Select the firmware load file for TNP 7970 phones
  7971        Select the firmware load file for TNP 7971 phones
  7975        Select the firmware load file for TNP 7975 phones
  ATA         Select the firmware load file for ATA

CME_ROUTER(config-register-global)#load 7942 SIP42.8-4-2S
CME_ROUTER(config-register-global)#authenticate register
CME_ROUTER(config-register-global)#tftp-path flash:
CME_ROUTER(config-register-global)#create profile
CME_ROUTER(config-register-global)#exit
```

Create profile command generates provisioning files required for SIP phones and writes the file to the location specified with the *tftp-path* command.

To make a successfull call between IP phones, we need to register the phones and create associations with the directory numbers. Dn (directory number) represents the line that connects a voice channel to IP phone, on which user can receive and make the calls. Dn is equivalent to a phone line in most cases. Each dn has a unique dn-tag, or a sequence number to identify it during configuration. In our configuration we create two dns, one for each IP phone. *Number* specifies the dial number to reach specific dn. *Name* is used to identify the caller IP phone.

CME_ROUTER config (ch7c3):

```
CME_ROUTER#configure terminal
CME_ROUTER(config)#voice register dn 1
CME_ROUTER(config-register-dn)#number 1001
CME_ROUTER(config-register-dn)#name SIP 1001
CME_ROUTER(config-register-dn)#exit
CME_ROUTER(config)#voice register dn 2
CME_ROUTER(config-register-dn)#number 1002
CME_ROUTER(config-register-dn)#name SIP 1002
CME_ROUTER(config-register-dn)#exit
```

Voice register pool command followed by the pool-tag with upper limit defined by the *max-pool* command allows us to associate specific IP phone with the dn. For this purpose, we use the MAC address of the IP phone. We use the *username* command to assign an authentication credentials to the IP phone user. Codec and the type of the IP phone can be specified in this configuration. After we set all of the parameters, we need to create profile files by issuing the *create profile* command in voice register global. [33]

```
CME_ROUTER(config)#voice register pool 1
CME_ROUTER(config-register-pool)#id mac 10BD.0000.0001
CME_ROUTER(config-register-pool)#number 1 dn 1
CME_ROUTER(config-register-pool)#username 101 password 12345
CME_ROUTER(config-register-pool)#codec g711ulaw
CME_ROUTER(config-register-pool)#type 7942
CME_ROUTER(config-register-pool)#exit
CME_ROUTER(config)#voice register pool 2
CME_ROUTER(config-register-pool)#id mac 10BD.0000.0002
CME_ROUTER(config-register-pool)#number 1 dn 2
CME_ROUTER(config-register-pool)#username 102 password 12345
CME_ROUTER(config-register-pool)#codec g711ulaw
CME_ROUTER(config-register-pool)#type 7942
CME_ROUTER(config-register-pool)#exit

CME_ROUTER(config)#voice register global
CME_ROUTER(config-register-global)#create profile
CME_ROUTER(config-register-global)#exit
CME_ROUTER(config)#exit
```

After creating the profile, IP phones should reset and upgrade firmware, if not, use the factory reset.

- Unplug the power or Ethernet (PoE) cable from the IP phone, and then plug in the cable again. The IP phone starts its power up cycle.
- Press and hold # button until the Headset, Mute, and Speaker buttons begin to flash in sequence, release #.
- Press 123456789*0# within 60 seconds after the Headset, Mute, and Speaker buttons begin to flash.
- If you enter this key sequence correctly, the IP phone goes through the factory reset process.

To display all the configurations and register information, use the *show voiceregister all* command.

CME_ROUTER config (ch7c4):

```
CME_ROUTER#show voice register all

VOICE REGISTER GLOBAL
======================
CONFIG [Version=7.1]
======================
  Version 7.1
  Mode is cme
  Max-pool is 10
```

```
Max-dn is 30
Outbound-proxy is enabled and will use global configured value
Source-address is 172.16.1.1 port 5060
Load 7942 is SIP42.8-4-2S
Authenticate register
Time-format is 12
Date-format is M/D/Y
Time-zone is 5
Hold-alert is disabled
Mwi stutter is disabled
Mwi registration for full E.164 is disabled
Forwarding local is enabled
Privacy is enabled
Privacy-on-hold is disabled
Dst auto adjust is enabled
   start at Apr week 1 day Sun time 02:00
   stop  at Oct week 8 day Sun time 02:00
Max redirect number is 5
IP QoS DSCP:
   ef (the MS 6 bits, 46, in ToS, 0xB8) for media
   cs3 (the MS 6 bits, 24, in ToS, 0x60) for signal
   af41 (the MS 6 bits, 34, in ToS, 0x88) for video
   default (the MS 6 bits, 0, in ToS, 0x0) for service
Telnet Level: 0
Tftp path is flash:
Generate text file is disabled
Tftp files are created, current syncinfo 0003100429802826
OS79XX.TXT is not created
timeout interdigit 10
network-locale[0] US     (This is the default network locale for this box)
network-locale[1] US
network-locale[2] US
network-locale[3] US
network-locale[4] US
user-locale[0] US     (This is the default user locale for this box)
user-locale[1] US
user-locale[2] US
user-locale[3] US
user-locale[4] US


VOICE REGISTER DN
==================
Dn Tag 1
Config:
  Number is 1001
  Preference is 0
  Huntstop is disabled
  Name SIP phone1
  Auto answer is disabled
Dn Tag 2
Config:
  Number is 1002
  Preference is 0
  Huntstop is disabled
  Name SIP phone2
  Auto answer is disabled

VOICE REGISTER TEMPLATE
========================

VOICE REGISTER DIALPLAN
========================

VOICE REGISTER POOL
===================
Pool Tag 1
Config:
  Mac address is 10BD.0000.0001
  Type is 7942
  Number list 1 : DN 1
  Proxy Ip address is 0.0.0.0
  DTMF Relay is disabled
  Call Waiting is enabled
  DnD is disabled
  Busy trigger per button value is 0
  keep-conference is enabled
  username 101 password 12345
```

```
  kpml signal is enabled
  Transport type is udp
  service-control mechanism is supported
  registration Call ID is 10bd0000-00010002-c9535990-8dd136a2@172.16.1.12
  Privacy feature is not configured.
  Privacy button is disabled
  active primary line is: 1001

  contact IP address: 172.16.1.12 port 5060

Dialpeers created:

dial-peer voice 40003 voip
 destination-pattern 1001
 session target ipv4:172.16.1.12:5060
 session protocol sipv2
 digit collect kpml
 codec  g711ulaw bytes 160
 after-hours-exempt    FALSE

Statistics:
  Active registrations  : 1

  Total SIP phones registered: 1
  Total Registration Statistics
    Registration requests  : 1
    Registration success   : 1
    Registration failed    : 0
    unRegister requests    : 0
    unRegister success     : 0
    unRegister failed      : 0

Pool Tag 2
Config:
  Mac address is 10BD.0000.0002
  Type is 7942
  Number list 1 : DN 2
  Proxy Ip address is 0.0.0.0
  DTMF Relay is disabled
  Call Waiting is enabled
  DnD is disabled
  Busy trigger per button value is 0
  keep-conference is enabled
  username 102 password 12345
  kpml signal is enabled
  Transport type is udp
  service-control mechanism is supported
  registration Call ID is 10bd0000-00020002-03377602-8ededce3@172.16.1.11
  Privacy feature is not configured.
  Privacy button is disabled
  active primary line is: 1002

  contact IP address: 172.16.1.11 port 5060

Dialpeers created:

dial-peer voice 40005 voip
 destination-pattern 1002
 session target ipv4:172.16.1.11:5060
 session protocol sipv2
 digit collect kpml
 codec  g711ulaw bytes 160
 after-hours-exempt    FALSE

Statistics:
  Active registrations  : 1
  Total SIP phones registered: 1
  Total Registration Statistics
    Registration requests  : 1
    Registration success   : 1
    Registration failed    : 0
    unRegister requests    : 0
    unRegister success     : 0
    unRegister failed      : 0
```

After the correct registration, both IP phones should be displayed in the active registrations and they should be ready to use. We check the functionality by dialing the 1002 on the IP phone 1 (number 1001). IP phone 2 (number 1002) should ring and/or flash in sequence.

❖ IP Communicator

We will use pool 1 and pool 2 from the previous configuration. Cisco IP Communicator is a desktop based IP phone application. With microphone and headphones connected to the PC, IP Communicator can operate as an ordinary IP phone with CUCME. Required configuration parameter is the IP address of TFTP server in the IP Communicator's preferences. We use the TFTP IP address 172.16.1.1. Nevertheless we use SIP, we need to configure basic telephony-service settings. [16]

CME_ROUTER config (ch7c5):

```
CME_ROUTER#configure terminal
CME_ROUTER(config)#no telephony-service

CME_ROUTER(config)#telephony-service
CME_ROUTER(config-telephony)#ip source-address 172.16.1.1 port
2000
CME_ROUTER(config-telephony)#max-ephones 10
CME_ROUTER(config-telephony)#max-dn 30
CME_ROUTER(config-telephony)#exit
CME_ROUTER(config)#exit
```

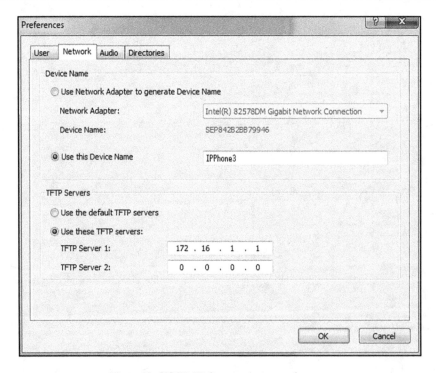

Figure 19: CISCO IP Communicator preferences

The IP Communicator has been registered as the ephone-1 (your registration may differ). We need to create an ephone-dn and associate it with the ephone-1.

```
CME_ROUTER#show ephone

ephone-1[0] Mac:842B.2BB7.9946 TCP socket:[1] activeLine:0 whisperLine:0
REGISTERED in SCCP ver 9/9 max_streams=3
mediaActive:0 whisper_mediaActive:0 startMedia:0 offhook:0 ringing:0 reset:0
reset_sent:0 paging 0 debug:0 caps:7
IP:172.16.5.10 49580 CIPC  keepalive 4 max_line 8 available_line 8
Preferred Codec: g711ulaw

CME_ROUTER#configure terminal
CME_ROUTER(config)#ephone-dn 1
CME_ROUTER(config-ephone-dn)#number 1003
CME_ROUTER(config-ephone-dn)#exit
CME_ROUTER(config)#ephone 1
CME_ROUTER(config-ephone)#mac-address 842B.2BB7.9946
CME_ROUTER(config-ephone)#button 1:1
CME_ROUTER(config-ephone)#restart
CME_ROUTER(config-ephone)#exit
CME_ROUTER(config)#exit
```

We can test the successful configuration by dialing the SIP pool 1 (1001) or pool 2 (1002) from the IP Communicator.

❖ Further study

Further study of the following subjects is strongly advised.

- SIP
- CUCME SIP overview
- TFTP

❖ Show running-config

CME_ROUTER running-config without IP Communicator:

```
hostname CME_ROUTER
no aaa new-model
memory-size iomem 25
dot11 syslog
ip source-route
ip cef
no ipv6 cef
multilink bundle-name authenticated
voice service voip
 allow-connections sip to sip
 sip
  registrar server expires max 1200 min 300
voice register global
 mode cme
 source-address 172.16.1.1 port 5060
 max-dn 30
 max-pool 10
 load 7942 SIP42.8-4-2S
 authenticate register
 tftp-path flash:
 create profile sync 0008224145072382
voice register dn  1
 number 1001
 name SIP phone1
voice register dn  2
 number 1002
 name SIP phone2
voice register pool  1
 id mac 10BD.0000.0001
 type 7942
 number 1 dn 1
 username 101 password 12345
 codec g711ulaw
voice register pool  2
 id mac 10BD.0000.0002
 type 7942
 number 1 dn 2
 username 102 password 12345
 codec g711ulaw
interface FastEthernet0/0
 no ip address
 duplex auto
 speed auto
interface FastEthernet0/0.5
 description ADMIN
 encapsulation dot1Q 5 native
 ip address 172.16.0.1 255.255.255.0
interface FastEthernet0/0.10
 description VLAN
```

```
 encapsulation dot1Q 10
 ip address 172.16.1.1 255.255.255.0
 ip helper-address 172.16.5.254
interface FastEthernet0/0.50
 description DATA
 encapsulation dot1Q 50
 ip address 172.16.5.1 255.255.255.0
interface FastEthernet0/1
 no ip address
 shutdown
 duplex auto
 speed auto
interface Serial0/0/0
 no ip address
 shutdown
 no fair-queue
 clock rate 125000
interface Serial0/0/1
 no ip address
 shutdown
interface Serial0/1/0
 no ip address
 shutdown
 clock rate 125000
interface Serial0/1/1
 no ip address
 shutdown
router rip
 version 2
 network 172.16.0.0
ip forward-protocol nd
no ip http server
no ip http secure-server
tftp-server flash:apps42.8-4-1-23.sbn
tftp-server flash:cnu42.8-4-1-23.sbn
tftp-server flash:cvm42sip.8-4-1-23.sbn
tftp-server flash:dsp42.8-4-1-23.sbn
tftp-server flash:jar42sip.8-4-1-23.sbn
tftp-server flash:SIP42.8-4-2S.loads
tftp-server flash:term42.default.loads
tftp-server flash:term62.default.loads
control-plane
line con 0
line aux 0
line vty 0 4
 login
 transport input all
scheduler allocate 20000 1000
end
```

❖ Quiz

1. SIP is proprietary protocol.

    A. Yes
    B. No

Answer: B

2. How many firmware files are required for a successful IP phone registration?

    A. 5
    B. 2
    C. It is IP phone type related
    D. None

Answer: C

3. Does CUCME need to be reinstalled to migrate from the SCCP to the SIP?

    A. Yes
    B. No
    C. No, but plugin needs to be installed instead

Answer: B

4. Which file will be sent to an un-configured Cisco IP phone by TFTP?

    A. XMLDefault.cnf.xml
    B. Firmware.xmf
    C. MAC address copy
    D. None

Answer: A

5. Which command sets the maximum number of pools?

    A. max-pool
    B. allowed pools
    C. pools-max-value
    D. show pool totals

Answer: A

"Intentionally blank"

BASIC CONFIGURATION SIP

CHAPTER 8

Chapter 8: BASIC CONFIGURATION SIP

The following chapter presents the basic CUCME configuration of directory numbers, pools and system settings that are essential for more advanced setup. We will explain how to assign directory numbers and how to overcome multiple problems associated with this process.

❖ Directory numbers and pools

❖ Shared line

❖ Template

❖ Time and date

❖ Description and Name

❖ Further study

❖ Quiz

❖ Directory numbers and pools

The initial topology and configuration of the network for this chapter stays the same as in the previous chapter. We additionally connect three more IP phones to the SWITCH_B, ports fa0/3-5. Total number of five IP phones allows us to test more complex scenarios. In case we use previous configurations, we need to wipe clean voice register configuration on CME_ROUTER. *No voice register global* command is the best option for this task. All the dns and pools must be removed before we issue the *no voice register global* command. It is a necessary step, if you are using configuration from the previous chapter. [33]

CME_ROUTER config (ch8c1):

```
CME_ROUTER#configure terminal

CME_ROUTER(config)#no telephony-service

CME_ROUTER(config)#no voice register dn 1
CME_ROUTER(config)#no voice register dn 2
CME_ROUTER(config)#no voice register pool 1
CME_ROUTER(config)#no voice register pool 2

CME_ROUTER(config)#no voice register global
Do you want to wipe out SIP CME config? [yes/no]: yes
CME_ROUTER(config)#exit
```

We also need to re-enable a voice register and configure basic parameters as follows.

CME_ROUTER config (ch8c2):

```
CME_ROUTER#configure terminal
CME_ROUTER(config)#voice register global
CME_ROUTER(config-register-global)#mode cme
CME_ROUTER(config-register-global)#source-address 172.16.1.1 port
5060
CME_ROUTER(config-register-global)#max-dn 30
CME_ROUTER(config-register-global)#max-pool 10
CME_ROUTER(config-register-global)#load 7942 SIP42.8-4-2S
CME_ROUTER(config-register-global)#authenticate register
CME_ROUTER(config-register-global)#tftp-path flash:
CME_ROUTER(config-register-global)#create profile
CME_ROUTER(config-register-global)#exit
CME_ROUTER(config)#exit
```

Initially, we will use three dns. All of them are configured as a default single-line directory numbers. A dual-line and an octo-line functionality are not supported by SIP.

Chapter 8: BASIC CONFIGURATION SIP

CME_ROUTER config (ch8c3):

```
CME_ROUTER#configure terminal
CME_ROUTER(config)#voice register dn 1
CME_ROUTER(config-register-dn)#number 1001
CME_ROUTER(config-register-dn)#name SIP 1001
CME_ROUTER(config-register-dn)#exit
CME_ROUTER(config)#voice register dn 2
CME_ROUTER(config-register-dn)#number 1002
CME_ROUTER(config-register-dn)#name SIP 1002
CME_ROUTER(config-register-dn)#exit
CME_ROUTER(config)#voice register dn 3
CME_ROUTER(config-register-dn)#number 1003
CME_ROUTER(config-register-dn)#name SIP 1003
CME_ROUTER(config-register-dn)#exit
```

We create three pools to associate dns with three IP phones. The first one will associate dn 1 with the button 1 on the IP phone (pool 1, mac address 10BD.0000.0001). The second one will associate dn 2 with the button 1 on the IP phone (pool 2, mac address 10BD.0000.0002) and the third one will associate dn 3 with the button 1 on the IP phone (pool 3, mac address 10BD.0000.0003) We leave the rest of the IP phones without dns association for the moment.

```
CME_ROUTER(config)#voice register pool 1
CME_ROUTER(config-register-pool)#id mac 10BD.0000.0001
CME_ROUTER(config-register-pool)#number 1 dn 1
CME_ROUTER(config-register-pool)#username 101 password 12345
CME_ROUTER(config-register-pool)#codec g711ulaw
CME_ROUTER(config-register-pool)#type 7942
CME_ROUTER(config-register-pool)#exit
CME_ROUTER(config)#voice register pool 2
CME_ROUTER(config-register-pool)#id mac 10BD.0000.0002
CME_ROUTER(config-register-pool)#number 1 dn 2
CME_ROUTER(config-register-pool)#username 102 password 12345
CME_ROUTER(config-register-pool)#codec g711ulaw
CME_ROUTER(config-register-pool)#type 7942
CME_ROUTER(config-register-pool)#exit
CME_ROUTER(config)#voice register pool 3
CME_ROUTER(config-register-pool)#id mac 10BD.0000.0003
CME_ROUTER(config-register-pool)#number 1 dn 3
CME_ROUTER(config-register-pool)#username 103 password 12345
CME_ROUTER(config-register-pool)#codec g711ulaw
CME_ROUTER(config-register-pool)#type 7942
CME_ROUTER(config-register-pool)#exit

CME_ROUTER(config)#voice register global
CME_ROUTER(config-register-global)#create profile
CME_ROUTER(config-register-global)#exit
CME_ROUTER(config)#exit
```

Here are three test scenarios for new configuration:

No. 1	dial	headset	ring	button 1	button 2
pool 1		flashes red	rings	flashes orange	off
pool 2		off	off	off	off
pool 3	1001	off	dial tone	green	off

No. 2	dial	headset	ring	button 1	button 2
pool 1		off	off	off	off
pool 2	1003	off	dial tone	green	off
pool 3		flashes red	rings	flashes orange	off

No. 3	dial	headset	ring	button 1	button 2
pool 1	1002	off	dial tone	green	off
pool 2		flashes red	rings	flashes orange	off
pool 3		off	off	off	off

❖ Shared line

We can create a shared line by assigning the same dn to the multiple IP phones. Not all IP phones support SIP shared-line (you should check the vendor documentation). The same directory number will display on multiple IP phones. An incoming call to number 1111 will ring simultaneously on the IP phone (pool 4, mac address 10BD.0000.0004) and IP phone (pool 5, mac address 10BD.0000.0005). The IP phone that answers first gets the call. The problem is that only one call can use the shared line at the time. The rest of the IP phones display the shared line as if it were in use.

CME_ROUTER config (ch8c4):

```
CME_ROUTER#configure terminal
CME_ROUTER(config)#voice register dn 11
CME_ROUTER(config-register-dn)#number 1111
CME_ROUTER(config-register-dn)#shared-line max-calls ?
<2-16>  Number of active calls supported on shared-line
CME_ROUTER(config-register-dn)#shared-line max-calls 2
CME_ROUTER(config-register-dn)#name SIP Shared
CME_ROUTER(config-register-dn)#exit

CME_ROUTER(config)#voice register pool 4
CME_ROUTER(config-register-pool)#id mac 10BD.0000.0004
CME_ROUTER(config-register-pool)#number 1 dn 11
CME_ROUTER(config-register-pool)#username 104 password 12345
CME_ROUTER(config-register-pool)#codec g711ulaw
CME_ROUTER(config-register-pool)#type 7942
CME_ROUTER(config-register-pool)#exit
CME_ROUTER(config)#voice register pool 5
CME_ROUTER(config-register-pool)#id mac 10BD.0000.0005
CME_ROUTER(config-register-pool)#number 1 dn 11
CME_ROUTER(config-register-pool)#user 105 password 12345
```

```
CME_ROUTER(config-register-pool)#codec g711ulaw
CME_ROUTER(config-register-pool)#type 7942
CME_ROUTER(config-register-pool)#exit

CME_ROUTER(config)#voice register global
CME_ROUTER(config-register-global)#create profile
CME_ROUTER(config-register-global)#exit
CME_ROUTER(config)#exit
```

We can test this scenario by dialing the directory number 1111 on pool 1.

No. 1	dial	headset	ring	button 1	button 2
pool 1	1111	off	dial tone	green	off
pool 4		flashes red	rings	flashes orange	off
pool 5		flashes red	rings	flashes orange	off

We answer the call on the IP phone (pool 4, mac address 10BD.0000.0004) and keep the call active. We dial the directory number 1111 on the IP phone (pool 2, mac address 10BD.0000.0002).

No. 2	dial	headset	ring	button 1	button 2
pool 2	1111	off	dial tone	green	off
pool 1	in call	active	off	green	off
pool 4		off	off	green	off
pool 5		red	rings	flashes orange	off

We answer the call on the IP phone (pool 5, mac address 10BD.0000.0005) and keep the call active. The Pool 1 is in active call with the pool 4 and the pool 2 is in active call with the pool 5. Max-calls parameter is set to the value 2. If we call directory number 1111 on IP phone (pool 3, mac address 10BD.0000.0003), we will get a busy tone.

We erase shared dn 11 and pools 4 and 5 to prepare for the next configuration.

CME_ROUTER config (ch8c5):

```
CME_ROUTER#configure terminal
CME_ROUTER(config)#no voice register dn 11
CME_ROUTER(config)#no voice register pool 4
CME_ROUTER(config)#no voice register pool 5

CME_ROUTER(config)#voice register global
CME_ROUTER(config-register-global)#create profile
CME_ROUTER(config-register-global)#exit
CME_ROUTER(config)#exit
```

The problem with a single directory number shared among the multiple dns can be solved by assigning the same directory number to the multiple dns.

CME_ROUTER config (ch8c6):

```
CME_ROUTER#configure terminal
CME_ROUTER(config)#voice register dn 11
CME_ROUTER(config-register-dn)#number 1111
CME_ROUTER(config-register-dn)#name SIP Shared
CME_ROUTER(config-register-dn)#exit
CME_ROUTER(config)#voice register dn 12
CME_ROUTER(config-register-dn)#number 1111
CME_ROUTER(config-register-dn)#name SIP Shared
CME_ROUTER(config-register-dn)#exit

CME_ROUTER(config)#voice register pool 4
CME_ROUTER(config-register-pool)#id mac 10BD.0000.0004
CME_ROUTER(config-register-pool)#number 1 dn 11
CME_ROUTER(config-register-pool)#username 104 password 12345
CME_ROUTER(config-register-pool)#codec g711ulaw
CME_ROUTER(config-register-pool)#type 7942
CME_ROUTER(config-register-pool)#exit
CME_ROUTER(config)#voice register pool 5
CME_ROUTER(config-register-pool)#id mac 10BD.0000.0005
CME_ROUTER(config-register-pool)#number 1 dn 12
CME_ROUTER(config-register-pool)#user 105 password 12345
CME_ROUTER(config-register-pool)#codec g711ulaw
CME_ROUTER(config-register-pool)#type 7942
CME_ROUTER(config-register-pool)#exit

CME_ROUTER(config)#voice register global
CME_ROUTER(config-register-global)#create profile
CME_ROUTER(config-register-global)#exit
CME_ROUTER(config)#exit
```

If the IP phones (pool 4, mac address 10BD.0000.0004 and pool 5, 10BD.0000.0005) do not restart, use the factory reset of the phones.

Now, we can test the same scenario by dialing the directory number 1111 on IP phone (pool 1, mac address 10BD.0000.0001). Pool 4 or pool 5 will ring. The problem is that the ring out is completely random. We can gain the control over how the call is delivered with the use of *preference* command. We can assign a preference value from 0 to 10, where lower values represent higher priority. The preference 0 is the default value. [19]

```
CME_ROUTER#configure terminal
CME_ROUTER(config)#voice register dn 11
CME_ROUTER(config-register-dn)# preference 5
CME_ROUTER(config-register-dn)#exit
CME_ROUTER(config)#voice register dn 12
CME_ROUTER(config-register-dn)# preference 1
CME_ROUTER(config-register-dn)#exit
CME_ROUTER(config)#exit
```

Now we can test the same scenario by dialing the directory number 1111 on IP phone (pool 1, mac address 10BD.0000.0001). Now all the calls to number 1111 are directed primarily to the IP phone (pool 5, mac address 10BD.0000.0005).

No. 1	dial	headset	ring	button 1	button 2
pool 1	1111	off	dial tone	green	off
pool 4	⨯	off	off	off	off
pool 5	⨯	flashes red	rings	flashes orange	off

We answer the call on pool 5 and keep the call active. We dial the directory number 1111 on IP phone (pool 2, mac address 10BD.0000.0002). A secondary incoming call to 1111, with primary call still active will not roll over to IP phone (pool 4, mac address 10BD.0000.0004), instead it will be received via call waiting on IP phone (pool 5, mac address 10BD.0000.0005). This situation can be handled with *huntstop* command. *Huntstop channel* tells the CME_ROUTER to stop hunting for other channel on the same IP phone.

```
CME_ROUTER#configure terminal
CME_ROUTER(config)#voice register dn 11
CME_ROUTER(config-register-dn)#huntstop channel 1
CME_ROUTER(config-register-dn)#exit

CME_ROUTER(config)#voice register dn 12
CME_ROUTER(config-register-dn)# huntstop channel 1
CME_ROUTER(config-register-dn)#exit
CME_ROUTER(config)#exit
```

The primary call to directory number 1111 is delivered to IP phone (pool 5, mac address 10BD.0000.0005). If the primary call is answered, the secondary call to directory number 1111 is delivered to the IP phone (pool 4, mac address 10BD.0000.0004). All the other calls to directory number 1111 will receive a busy signal.

❖ Template

We can pass multiple configuration parameters to the IP phone by creating the template. The template can be subsequently applied to the multiple IP phones using the *voice register template* command. We can define multiple different templates, but we cannot apply more than one template to a single pool. The following example illustrates the use of *template* command to modify the order of soft keys. We will create a template 1 and assign it to the pool 2. [34]

CME_ROUTER config (ch8c7):

```
CME_ROUTER#configure terminal

CME_ROUTER(config)#voice register template ?
<1-10>  voice-register-temp tag
CME_ROUTER(config)#voice register template 1
```

```
CME_ROUTER(config-register-temp)#softkeys ?
connected       Softkey order for connected state
hold            Softkey order for HOLD state
idle            Softkey order for IDLE state
remote-in-use   Softkey order for remote-in-use state
ringIn          Softkey order for RingIn state
seized          Softkey order for seized state

CME_ROUTER(config-register-temp)#softkeys ringIn ?
Answer   Answer
DND      Do Not Disturb
<cr>
CME_ROUTER(config-register-temp)#softkeys ringIn DND Answer
CME_ROUTER(config-register-temp)#exit

CME_ROUTER(config)#voice register pool 2
CME_ROUTER(config-register-pool)#template 1
CME_ROUTER(config-register-pool)#exit
CME_ROUTER(config)#voice register global
CME_ROUTER(config-register-global)#create profile
CME_ROUTER(config-register-global)#exit
CME_ROUTER(config)#voice register pool 2
CME_ROUTER(config-register-pool)#restart
CME_ROUTER(config-register-pool)#exit
CME_ROUTER(config)#exit
```

Now we can test the same scenario by dialing the directory number 1002 on the IP phone (pool 1, mac address 10BD.0000.0001). As we can see, the template was applied (Figure 20).

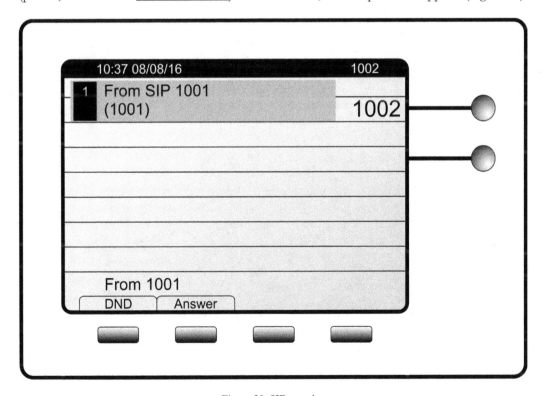

Figure 20: SIP template

❖ Time and date

The time and date format displayed on the IP phones can be modified with the *date-format* and *time-format* commands. [22]

CME_ROUTER config (ch8c8):

```
CME_ROUTER#configure terminal
CME_ROUTER(config)#voice register global
CME_ROUTER(config-register-global)#date-format ?
D/M/Y    Set date to D/M/Y format
M/D/Y    Set date to M/D/Y format
Y-M-D    Set date to Y-M-D format
Y/D/M    Set date to Y/D/M format
Y/M/D    Set date to Y/M/D format
YY-M-D   Set date to YY-M-D format

CME_ROUTER(config-register-global)#date-format M/D/Y

CME_ROUTER(config-register-global)#time-format ?
12  Set time to 12Hrs(AM/PM) format
24  Set time to 24Hrs format

CME_ROUTER(config-register-global)#time-format 24
CME_ROUTER(config-register-global)#create profile
CME_ROUTER(config-register-global)#restart
CME_ROUTER(config-register-global)#exit
CME_ROUTER(config)#exit

CME_ROUTER#show clock
*15:19:04.646 UTC Mon Aug 08 2016

CME_ROUTER#configure terminal
CME_ROUTER(config)#voice register global
CME_ROUTER(config-register-global)#timezone ?
  <1-53>  select timezone name used by IP phones (offset in minutes)
1 Dateline Standard Time -720
2 Samoa Standard Time -660
3 Hawaiian Standard Time -600
4 Alaskan Standard/Daylight Time -540
5 Pacific Standard/Daylight Time -480
6 Mountain Standard/Daylight Time -420
7 US Mountain Standard Time -420
8 Central Standard/Daylight Time -360
9 Mexico Standard/Daylight Time -360
10 Canada Central Standard Time -360
.Omitted output
21 GMT Standard/Daylight Time +0
.Omitted output
53 New Zealand Standard/Daylight Time +720

CME_ROUTER(config-register-global)#timezone 21
CME_ROUTER(config-register-global)#create profile
CME_ROUTER(config-register-global)#restart
CME_ROUTER(config-register-global)#exit
CME_ROUTER(config)#exit
```

❖ Description, name and label

IP phone header bar description can be modified with *description* command. If the description is not specified, the header bar replicates the extension number that appears next to the first button on the IP phone. We use the *name* command to associate the name with the directory number. The name is displayed during an active call. The label is a text identifier which replaces a phone-number display for an extension on an IP phone console. The system message in cme mode is not supported. [23]

CME_ROUTER config (ch8c9):

```
CME_ROUTER#configure terminal
CME_ROUTER(config)#voice register pool 1
CME_ROUTER(config-register-pool)#description User1
CME_ROUTER(config-register-pool)#exit
CME_ROUTER(config)#voice register dn 1
CME_ROUTER(config-register-dn)#name SIP1001
CME_ROUTER(config-register-dn)#label SIP1001
CME_ROUTER(config-register-dn)#exit
CME_ROUTER(config)#voice register global
CME_ROUTER(config-register-global)#create profile
CME_ROUTER(config-register-global)#restart
CME_ROUTER(config-register-global)#exit
CME_ROUTER(config)#exit
```

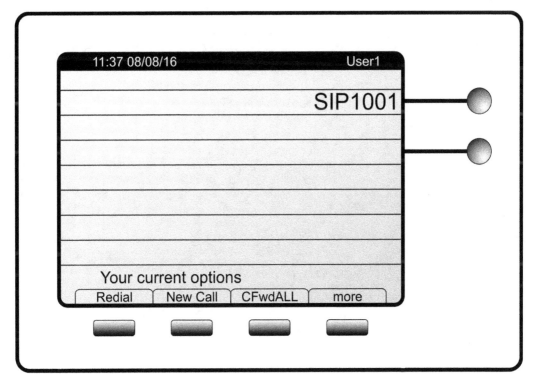

Figure 21: SIP description and label

❖ Further study

Further study of the following subjects is strongly advised.

- Template
- Softkeys

❖ **Quiz**

1. Which command can be used to modify the CUCME SIP system message?

   A. sysmod
   B. none, system message is not supported
   C. name
   D. label

   Answer: B

2. How many templates can be associated with a single pool?

   A. None
   B. One
   C. At least one
   D. It is limited by the version of CUCME.

   Answer: B

3. Which preference value represents a default dn priority?

   A. 1024
   B. 0
   C. master
   D. 1

   Answer: B

4. What is the best description of a shared line?

   A. List of pools
   B. Dn line splitter
   C. Distributed dn name
   D. Dn shared with the multiple pools

   Answer: D

5. Which command modifies the description of a header bar?

   A. description
   B. name
   C. header
   D. message

   Answer: A

"Intentionally blank"

ADVANCED CONFIGURATION SIP

CHAPTER 9

Chapter 9: ADVANCED CONFIGURATION SIP

In this chapter we present an advanced SIP configuration. Advanced functionality allows handling the call in more sophisticated way.

- ❖ Initial configuration
- ❖ Local directory
- ❖ Call forwarding
- ❖ Call transfer
- ❖ Call pickup
- ❖ Call parking
- ❖ Intercom
- ❖ Call blocking
- ❖ Music On Hold
- ❖ Further study
- ❖ Quiz

❖ Initial configuration

Initial topology of the network for this chapter stays the same as in the previous chapter. We setup two dns and two pools. We will add a few more of them later. You should use your IP phone *type* in the configuration. Initially we need to wipe a voice register configuration from the previous chapter. We assume that SIP firmware has already been loaded. If it was not, you should look at the previous chapter.

CME_ROUTER config (ch9c1):

```
CME_ROUTER#configure terminal
CME_ROUTER(config)#no voice register dn 1
CME_ROUTER(config)#no voice register dn 2
CME_ROUTER(config)#no voice register dn 3
CME_ROUTER(config)#no voice register dn 11
CME_ROUTER(config)#no voice register dn 12

CME_ROUTER(config)#no voice register pool 1
CME_ROUTER(config)#no voice register pool 2
CME_ROUTER(config)#no voice register pool 3
CME_ROUTER(config)#no voice register pool 4
CME_ROUTER(config)#no voice register pool 5

CME_ROUTER(config)#no voice register global
Do you want to wipe out SIP CME config? [yes/no]: yes
CME_ROUTER(config)#exit
```

CME_ROUTER config (ch9c2):

```
CME_ROUTER(config)#voice register global
CME_ROUTER(config-register-global)#mode cme
CME_ROUTER(config-register-global)#source-address 172.16.1.1 port
5060
CME_ROUTER(config-register-global)#max-dn 30
CME_ROUTER(config-register-global)#max-pool 10
CME_ROUTER(config-register-global)#exit

CME_ROUTER(config)#voice register dn 1
CME_ROUTER(config-register-dn)#number 1001
CME_ROUTER(config-register-dn)#name John Doe
CME_ROUTER(config-register-dn)#exit
CME_ROUTER(config)#voice register dn 2
CME_ROUTER(config-register-dn)#number 1002
CME_ROUTER(config-register-dn)#name Jane Doe
CME_ROUTER(config-register-dn)#exit

CME_ROUTER(config)#voice register pool 1
CME_ROUTER(config-register-pool)#id mac 10BD.0000.0001
CME_ROUTER(config-register-pool)#number 1 dn 1
CME_ROUTER(config-register-pool)#username 101 password 12345
CME_ROUTER(config-register-pool)#codec g711ulaw
CME_ROUTER(config-register-pool)#type 7942
```

```
CME_ROUTER(config-register-pool)#exit
CME_ROUTER(config)#voice register pool 2
CME_ROUTER(config-register-pool)#id mac 10BD.0000.0002
CME_ROUTER(config-register-pool)#number 1 dn 2
CME_ROUTER(config-register-pool)#username 102 password 12345
CME_ROUTER(config-register-pool)#codec g711ulaw
CME_ROUTER(config-register-pool)#type 7942
CME_ROUTER(config-register-pool)#exit

CME_ROUTER(config)#voice register global
CME_ROUTER(config-register-global)#create profile
CME_ROUTER(config-register-global)#exit
CME_ROUTER(config)#exit
```

❖ Local directory

Local directory is automatically created by CUCME and contains the numbers assigned in the dns. Local directory is accessible for each registered IP phone. Local directory includes all the dns created in CUCME. Manual directory entries are also allowed. The following configuration enables a http server on CME_ROUTER. It is a necessary step to allow IP phones to access Local directory folder. The URL of Local directory must be specified (http://172.16.1.1/localdirectory). [35]

CME_ROUTER config (ch9c3):

```
CME_ROUTER#configure terminal
CME_ROUTER(config)#ip http server

CME_ROUTER(config)#voice register global
CME_ROUTER(config-register-global)#url directory
http://172.16.1.1/localdirectory

CME_ROUTER(config-register-global)#create profile
CME_ROUTER(config-register-global)#restart
CME_ROUTER(config-register-global)#exit
CME_ROUTER(config)#exit
```

Local directory can be browsed by the IP phone user in the following way.

- Press *Directories* softkey on the IP phone.
- Select *Local directory*.
- Type the *First* or *Last* name. In case we leave the fields blank, all users in local directory will be displayed.

❖ Call forwarding

In the case we want to answer the call on the IP phone that is located elsewhere, we can use Call forwarding feature to direct the call from one IP phone to another. There are basically two types of the forwarding available. The first one is a user based dynamic call forwarding. The second one is static and can be configured directly on CUCME.

We need to add another IP phone to the existing configuration.

CME_ROUTER config (ch9c4):

```
CME_ROUTER#configure terminal
CME_ROUTER(config)#voice register dn 3
CME_ROUTER(config-register-dn)#number 1003
CME_ROUTER(config-register-dn)#name Frank Tableton
CME_ROUTER(config-register-dn)#exit

CME_ROUTER(config)#voice register pool 3
CME_ROUTER(config-register-pool)#id mac 10BD.0000.0003
CME_ROUTER(config-register-pool)#number 1 dn 3
CME_ROUTER(config-register-pool)#username 103 password 12345
CME_ROUTER(config-register-pool)#codec g711ulaw
CME_ROUTER(config-register-pool)#type 7942
CME_ROUTER(config-register-pool)#exit

CME_ROUTER(config)#voice register global
CME_ROUTER(config-register-global)#create profile
CME_ROUTER(config-register-global)#restart
CME_ROUTER(config-register-global)#exit
CME_ROUTER(config)#exit
```

Dynamic call forwarding

We press *CFwdAll* softkey on the on IP phone (pool 3, mac address 10BD.0000.0003). The IP phone is waiting for a new number, where all the calls will be forwarded. After we enter 1002, we press the *EndCall* softkey. Home screen is displayed immediately with the "Forwarded to 1002" message. Now if we dial 1003 from IP phone (pool 1, mac address 10BD.0000.0001). The call is automatically forwarded to the pool 2. We can cancel the call forwarding by pressing the *CFwdAll* softkey on pool 3. Message "Forwarded to 1002" disappears. [25]

Static call forwarding

Static call forwarding has more options than its dynamic version. Static forwarding can be overridden, using the dynamic call forwarding.

CME_ROUTER config (ch9c5):

```
CME_ROUTER#configure terminal
CME_ROUTER(config)#voice register dn 3
CME_ROUTER(config-register-dn)#call-forward b2bua ?
all       forward all calls
busy      forward call on busy
mailbox   mailbox number
noan      forward call on no-answer

CME_ROUTER(config-register-dn)#call-forward b2bua noan 1002
timeout 10
CME_ROUTER(config-register-dn)#exit

CME_ROUTER(config)#voice register global
CME_ROUTER(config-register-global)#create profile
CME_ROUTER(config-register-global)#restart
CME_ROUTER(config-register-global)#exit
CME_ROUTER(config)#exit
```

If we call 1003 from an IP phone (pool 1, mac address 10BD.0000.0001) and do not answer, the call is forwarded to pool 2 after 10 seconds.

❖ Call transfer

Call transfer moves the active call from one number to another. On the IP phone, we perform this task by pressing the *Transfer* softkey and dialing the number where we forward the call. Call is immediately forwarded. We can test this scenario by dialing the 1002 from IP phone (pool 1, mac address 10BD.0000.0001), answering the call and use the *Transfer* softkey to transfer the call to 1003. The call is immediately transferred to the pool 3.

❖ Call pickup

Call pickup allows a user to answer the remote extension on the local IP phone. Before we can use a Call pickup feature we need to define *pickup-call* and *pickup-group*. We can assign each dn to only one pickup-group and dn must have a pickup-group configured. *Pickup-call any-group* enables a user to pick up ringing calls on any extension belonging to the pickup group. PickUp softkey does the trick. We dial 1003 from the IP phone (pool 1, mac address 10BD.0000.0001) to reach the IP phone (pool 3, mac address 10BD.0000.0003). While the IP phone (pool 3, mac address 10BD.0000.0003) is ringing, we press the Pickup softkey on the IP phone (pool 2, mac address 10BD.0000.0002) and enter the number 1003. Call is immediately picked and the IP phone (pool 3, mac address 10BD.0000.0003) stops ringing.

CME_ROUTER config (ch9c6):

```
CME_ROUTER#configure terminal
CME_ROUTER(config)#voice register dn 1
CME_ROUTER(config-register-dn)# allow watch
 pickup-call any-group
 pickup-group 1
 huntstop channel 1
 mwi
CME_ROUTER(config)#voice register dn 2
CME_ROUTER(config-register-dn)# allow watch
 pickup-call any-group
 pickup-group 1
 huntstop channel 1
 mwi
CME_ROUTER(config)#voice register dn 3
CME_ROUTER(config-register-dn)# allow watch
 pickup-call any-group
 pickup-group 1
 huntstop channel 1
 mwi

CME_ROUTER(config)#telephony-service
CME_ROUTER(config-telephony)#call-park system application
CME_ROUTER(config-telephony)#exit
```

❖ Call parking

Call parking allows us to park an active call. It has similar functionality as hold, except it is possible to resume the call from any IP phone. Additional ephone-dn has to be configured. It will serve as parking slot and will not be assigned to any button. We use *telephony-service* parking slot for SIP parking. [26]

CME_ROUTER config (ch9c7):

```
CME_ROUTER#configure terminal

CME_ROUTER(config)#no telephony-service

CME_ROUTER(config)#telephony-service
CME_ROUTER(config-telephony)#ip source-address 172.16.1.1 port
2000
CME_ROUTER(config-telephony)#max-ephones 10
CME_ROUTER(config-telephony)#max-dn 30
CME_ROUTER(config-telephony)#call-park system application

CME_ROUTER(config-telephony)#exit

CME_ROUTER(config)#ephone-dn 11
CME_ROUTER(config-ephone-dn)#number 1111
CME_ROUTER(config-ephone-dn)#name Parking
```

```
CME_ROUTER(config-ephone-dn)#park-slot
CME_ROUTER(config-ephone-dn)#exit
CME_ROUTER(config)#exit
```

To test the Call parking we dial 1003 from the IP phone (pool 1, mac address 10BD.0000.0001) to reach the IP phone (pool 3, mac address 10BD.0000.0003). We answer the call. With the call still active we use *Park* softkey on the IP phone (pool 3, mac address 10BD.0000.0003) to park the call to the park slot 1111. The IP phone (pool 1, mac address 10BD.0000.0001) displays message that the call is parked to 1111. We can pick up the call from the IP phone (pool 2, mac address 10BD.0000.0002) by dialing the number 1111.

❖ Intercom

The intercom is basically a dial with the automatic answer on loudspeaker. A microphone is unmuted by default. We set up a new dn for the intercom between two IP phones. We assign dn 15 to the second button of the IP phone (pool 2, mac address 10BD.0000.0002). [27]

CME_ROUTER config (ch9c8):

```
CME_ROUTER#configure terminal
CME_ROUTER(config)#voice register dn 15
CME_ROUTER(config-register-dn)#number 1015
CME_ROUTER(config-register-dn)#auto-answer
CME_ROUTER(config-register-dn)#exit

CME_ROUTER(config)#voice register pool 2
CME_ROUTER(config-register-pool)#number 2 dn 15
CME_ROUTER(config-register-pool)#exit

CME_ROUTER(config)#voice register global
CME_ROUTER(config-register-global)#create profile
CME_ROUTER(config-register-global)#restart
CME_ROUTER(config-register-global)#exit
CME_ROUTER(config)#exit
```

We can test the intercom by dialing the 1015 from the IP phone (pool 1, mac address 10BD.0000.0001). The call is auto-answered with an unmuted microphone. The intercom line cannot be the primary line of a SIP IP phone. And it cannot be shared among SIP IP phones.

❖ Call blocking

There are multiple ways how to block users from making the calls. Several restrictions can be applied to limit the access for specific users. Not everyone should be allowed to dial long – distance calls or use the IP phone after working hours. We can use *after-hours* command for call blocking based on time and dialing number. The following example shows how to block the calls based on specific time, date and the set of numbers. We use actual date and time to test the scenario.

CME_ROUTER config (ch9c9):

```
CME_ROUTER#show clock
*11:09:23.055 UTC Mon Feb 1 2016

CME_ROUTER#configure terminal
CME_ROUTER(config)#no telephony-service

CME_ROUTER(config)#telephony-service
CME_ROUTER(config-telephony)#ip source-address 172.16.1.1 port
2000
CME_ROUTER(config-telephony)#max-ephones 10
CME_ROUTER(config-telephony)#max-dn 30

CME_ROUTER(config-telephony)#after-hours day Mon 10:00 23:59
CME_ROUTER(config-telephony)#after-hours date Feb 29 00:00 23:59
CME_ROUTER(config-telephony)#after-hours block pattern 1 10..
CME_ROUTER(config-telephony)#exit
CME_ROUTER(config)#exit
```

Now, if we dial any number starting with 10 followed by two digits the call is immediately terminated. There is no pin to bypass blocking on SIP IP phones. However, we can exempt all extensions associated with an individual SIP IP phone or an individual directory number from the Call Blocking configuration. [36]

CME_ROUTER config (ch9c10):

```
CME_ROUTER#confure terminal
CME_ROUTER(config)#voice register pool 1
CME_ROUTER(config-register-pool)#after-hour exempt
CME_ROUTER(config-register-pool)#exit

CME_ROUTER(config)#voice register pool 2
CME_ROUTER(config-register-dn)#after-hour exempt
CME_ROUTER(config-register-dn)#exit

CME_ROUTER(config)#voice register global
CME_ROUTER(config-register-global)#create profile
CME_ROUTER(config-register-global)#restart
CME_ROUTER(config-register-global)#exit
CME_ROUTER(config)#exit
```

If we dial 1002 from the IP phone (pool 1, mac address 10BD.0000.0001), it will ring and we can answer the call. Same applies for the call form the IP phone (pool 2, mac address 10BD.0000.0002) to the IP phone (pool 1, mac address 10BD.0000.0001). However, if we try to reach any pool from the IP phone (pool 3, mac address 10BD.0000.0003) the call is immediately terminated because of after-hour blocking. It is also possible to block selected numbers 24-7. We can test this by blocking the number 1003.

```
CME_ROUTER#confure terminal
CME_ROUTER(config)#voice register pool 1
CME_ROUTER(config-register-pool)#no after-hour
CME_ROUTER(config-register-pool)#exit

CME_ROUTER(config)#voice register pool 2
CME_ROUTER(config-register-dn)#no after-hour
CME_ROUTER(config-register-dn)#exit

CME_ROUTER(config)#no telephony-service

CME_ROUTER(config)#telephony-service
CME_ROUTER(config-telephony)#ip source-address 172.16.1.1 port
2000
CME_ROUTER(config-telephony)#max-ephones 10
CME_ROUTER(config-telephony)#max-dn 30

Router(config-telephony)#after-hours block pattern 3 1003 7-24
CME_ROUTER(config-telephony)#exit
CME_ROUTER(config)#exit
```

If we call the directory number 1003 from any IP phone we get the busy tone 24-7. All the blocking restrictions can be canceled by entering the *no* form of *after-hours* command.

❖ Music On Hold

Music on hold plays the music file while the caller is on hold. It makes the waiting less painful and users know that they waiting for the call and have not been disconnected. Music files have to be stored on the router flash and they have to follow some rules to be successfully played during the hold. We can copy music files to the router flash using the TFTP server. The process of copying files over TFTP has already been presented, or we can use a CompactFlash card reader to copy music files to the flash. The list of files included on the flash can be displayed using *show flash:* command. As we can see, our flash has music-on-hold.au file on it. Compatible music files must have the following requirements:

- *au* or *wav* file format

- G.711 codec

- 8-bit rate at 8kHz

- be careful with the copyrighted music [30]

CME_ROUTER config (ch9c11):

```
CME_ROUTER#show flash:
*Feb  8 12:04:09.663: %SYS-5-CONFIG_I: Configured from console by console
-#- --length-- -----date/time------ path
Omitted output
10       496521 Feb 08 2016 00:52:18 music-on-hold.au
```

Music on hold can be distributed as a unicast or multicast stream. Music on hold is configured if *multicast* command is not included. Unicast streaming consumes a notable amount of bandwidth. Multicast is a more efficient solution. However, it is not usable in the scenarios with multiple subnets. In that case, unicast is the only choice.

```
CME_ROUTER#confure terminal
CME_ROUTER(config)#telephony-service
CME_ROUTER(config-telephony)#moh music-on-hold.au
CME_ROUTER(config-telephony)# multicast moh 239.25.5.15 port 2000
CME_ROUTER(config-telephony)#restart all
CME_ROUTER(config)#exit
```

We can test the configuration by dialing 1001 from the IP phone (pool 2, mac address 10BD.0000.0002). We answer the call on the IP phone (pool 1, mac address 10BD.0000.0001) and put it on hold. Music on hold should play on the IP phone (pool 2, mac address 10BD.0000.0002).

❖ Further study

CUCME contains more advanced services and functions. If the set presented in this chapter does not contain service or function you are looking for, further study is advised.

❖ Quiz

1. Which audio format is compatible with the music on hold?

   A. gif2000
   B. au
   C. uc
   D. mp4

   Answer: B

2. Intercom is answered

   A. on loudspeaker.
   B. and inserted to the block list.
   C. and transferred immediately.
   D. after 5 second ring out.

   Answer: A

3. Call pickup allows user

   A. to choose among the multiple call slots.
   B. to check the mailbox.
   C. to answer the remote extension.
   D. to list the missed calls.

   Answer: C

4. What is required for a proper function of the call parking?

   A. Ephone-dn park-slot
   B. SIP slot
   C. Parking softkey
   D. Parking MAC address

   Answer: A

5. Choose the correct command for nonstop blocking of dn 1003.

   A. block pattern 3 1003 permanent
   B. after-hours block pattern 1 1003 24-7
   C. after-hours block pattern 3 1003 7-24
   D. call transfer 1003 blocklst
   E. deny 1003 nonstop

   Answer: C

"Intentionally blank"

HYBRID CONFIGURATION SCCP/ SIP

CHAPTER 10

Chapter 10: HYBRID CONFIGURATION SCCP / SIP

Slightly modified functional topology and configuration presented in the chapter 2 is required for this chapter. We will use two IP phones and one PC with an IP Communicator. The rest of the topology and configuration stays the same as in the chapter 2. We will combine SCCP and SIP protocols to create the hybrid configuration. Both protocols can co-exist and cooperate in one CUCME. We will start with the SCCP and then we add the SIP. Reverse approach is also possible.

❖ Network topology scheme

❖ Hardware requirements

❖ SCCP

❖ IP Communicator

❖ SIP

❖ Further study

❖ Quiz

❖ **Network topology scheme**

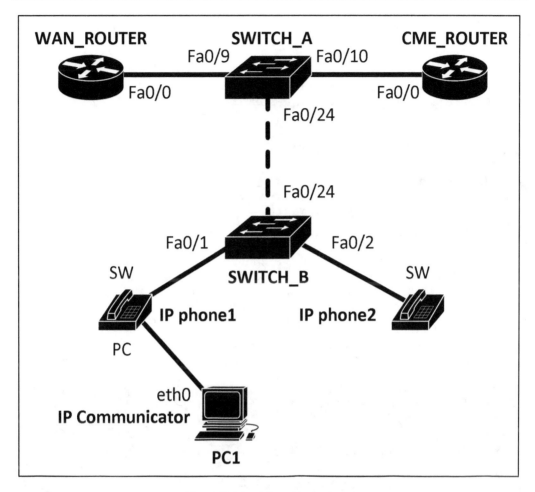

Figure 22: Network topology scheme

❖ **Hardware requirements**

2x Router (WAN_ROUTER, CME_ROUTER)
2x Switch (SWITCH_A, SWITCH_B)
2x IP phone (IP phone1, IP phone2)
1x PC (PC1)
5x Straight cable
1x Cross-over cable

❖ SCCP

Firstly, we need to enable *telephony-service* and define basic parameters.

CME_ROUTER config (ch10c1):

```
CME_ROUTER#configure terminal
CME_ROUTER(config)#no telephony-service

CME_ROUTER(config)#telephony-service
CME_ROUTER(config-telephony)#ip source-address 172.16.1.1 port
2000
CME_ROUTER(config-telephony)#max-ephones 10
CME_ROUTER(config-telephony)#max-dn 30
CME_ROUTER(config-telephony)#exit
CME_ROUTER(config)#exit
```

Now, we need to download SCCP and SIP firmware files for IP phones. SCCP and SIP firmware files for the same type of IP phone differ. Search the IP phone vendor site for firmware files. We use TFTP to upload files to the CME_ROUTER and decompress it on the place. We use PC1 for this purpose. We need to check IP address of PC1. It was delivered by WAN_ROUTER from DHCP data pool. One option is to use *ipconfig* in a command line window. PC1 received IP address 172.16.5.10, your PC could and, almost surely, received different IP address, but it has to be from the same DHCP data pool.

```
C:\Users\cisco>ipconfig

Windows IP Configuration


Ethernet adapter Ethernet:

   Connection-specific DNS Suffix  . :
   Link-local IPv6 Address . . . . . : fe80::18b3:3e67:c90:1438%3
   IPv4 Address. . . . . . . . . . . : 172.16.5.10
   Subnet Mask . . . . . . . . . . . : 255.255.255.0
   Default Gateway . . . . . . . . . : 172.16.5.254
```

Figure 23: PC IP configuration

We check the reachability of PC1 with the *ping* command executed on CME_ROUTER.

CME_ROUTER config (ch10c2):

```
CME_ROUTER#ping 172.16.5.10
Type escape sequence to abort.
Sending 5, 100-byte ICMP Echos to 172.16.5.10, timeout is 2 seconds:
.!!!!
Success rate is 100 percent (5/5), round-trip min/avg/max = 1/1/1 ms
```

We download and run TFTP software of your choice on PC1. All we need to do is run the software and choose the directory where the tar firmware file is located. Also correct network interface has to be selected. (fig. 23)

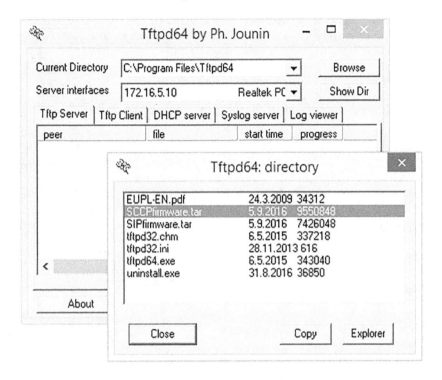

Figure 24: PC TFTP server SCCP

In next step, we download and extract SCCP firmware files to the flash card of CME_ROUTER.

CME_ROUTER config (ch10c3):

```
CME_ROUTER#archive tar /xtract
tftp://172.16.5.10/SCCPfirmware.tar flash:
Loading IPphonefirmware.tar from 172.16.5.10 (via FastEthernet0/0.50): !
extracting apps42.9-2-1TH1-13.sbn (4639974 bytes)!!!!!!!!!!!!!!!!!!!!
extracting cnu42.9-2-1TH1-13.sbn (575495 bytes)O!!
extracting cvm42sccp.9-2-1TH1-13.sbn (2208583 bytes)O!!!!!!!!!!
extracting dsp42.9-2-1TH1-13.sbn (356907 bytes)O!
extracting jar42sccp.9-2-1TH1-13.sbn (1759967 bytes)!!!!!!!!
extracting SCCP42.9-2-1S.loads (676 bytes)O
extracting term42.default.loads (680 bytes)
extracting term62.default.loads (680 bytes)
[OK - 9550848 bytes]
```

After a successful download and extraction all the files should be located on CME_ROUTER flash card. All the downloaded files have to be registered with the TFTP server (CME_ROUTER not PC1) to be reachable for the IP phone. *Tftp-server* command allows us to register the files.

CME_ROUTER config (ch10c4):

```
CME_ROUTER#configure terminal
CME_ROUTER(config)#tftp-server flash:apps42.9-2-1TH1-13.sbn
CME_ROUTER(config)#tftp-server flash:cnu42.9-2-1TH1-13.sbn
CME_ROUTER(config)#tftp-server flash:cvm42sccp.9-2-1TH1-13.sbn
CME_ROUTER(config)#tftp-server flash:dsp42.9-2-1TH1-13.sbn
CME_ROUTER(config)#tftp-server flash:jar42sccp.9-2-1TH1-13.sbn
CME_ROUTER(config)#tftp-server flash:SCCP42.9-2-1S.loads
CME_ROUTER(config)#tftp-server flash:term42.default.loads
CME_ROUTER(config)#tftp-server flash:term62.default.loads
```

After a successful TFTP registration, firmware needs to be associated with the specific type of the IP phone. If we use load command followed by the question mark, console displays all the supported types. The group of supported types depends on which IOS and CUCME is installed on the router. To build the XML configuration files that are required for IP phones in CUCME, we use the *create cnf-files* command. Now the IP phone should be able to download and install firmware.

```
CME_ROUTER(config)#telephony-service
CME_ROUTER(config-telephony)#load 7942 SCCP42.9-2-1S
CME_ROUTER(config-telephony)#create cnf-files
Creating CNF files...

CME_ROUTER(config-telephony)#exit
CME_ROUTER(config)#exit
```

Complete the following steps to perform factory reset of IP phone 1:

- Unplug the power or Ethernet (PoE) cable from the IP phone, and then plug in the cable again. The IP phone starts power up cycle.
- Press and hold # button while the Headset, Mute, and Speaker buttons begin to flash in sequence, release #.
- Press 123456789*0# within 60 seconds after the Headset, Mute, and Speaker buttons begin to flash.
- If you enter this key sequence correctly, the IP phone goes through the factory reset process.

IP phone should download SCCP firmware and register with the CUCME.

The following configuration registers physical IP phone 1 (MAC address 10BD.0000.0001) as ephone 1 and assigns ephone-dn 1 to its button 1. Your registration may differ, please check your ephone registration with *show ephone* command.

CME_ROUTER config (ch10c5):

```
CME_ROUTER(config)#ephone-dn 1
CME_ROUTER(config-ephone-dn)#number 1001
CME_ROUTER(config-ephone-dn)#exit
CME_ROUTER(config)#exit


CME_ROUTER#show ephone
ephone-1[0] Mac:10BD.0000.0001 TCP socket:[1] activeLine:0 whisperLine:0
REGISTERED in SCCP ver 20/12 max_streams=5
Omitted output

CME_ROUTER#configure terminal
CME_ROUTER(config)#ephone 1
CME_ROUTER(config-ephone)#mac-address 10BD.0000.0001
CME_ROUTER(config-ephone)#button 1:1
CME_ROUTER(config-ephone)#restart
CME_ROUTER(config-ephone)#exit
CME_ROUTER(config)#exit
```

❖ IP Communicator

We will use an IP Communicator as the second SCCP IP phone. Search the IP Communicator association with the *show ephone* command and compare mac address with the name displayed as a "Device Name" in IP Communicator preferences (Network tab). The IP Communicator has been registered as an ephone-3 (your registration may differ). Also your IP address may differ. We need to create ephone-dn and associate it with the ephone-3.

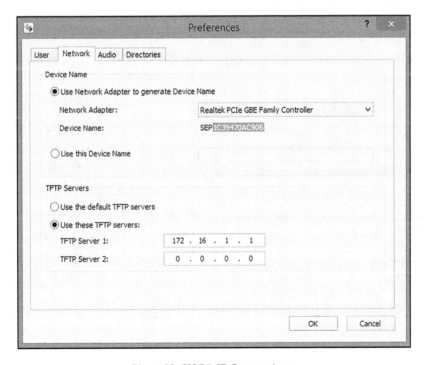

Figure 25: CISCO IP Communicator

We configure ephone-dn 3 with number 1003 and assign it to the first button on ephone 3. A successful registration requires configuring TFTP server 1 address 172.16.1.1 in network tab of IP Communicator preferences.

CME_ROUTER config (ch10c6):

```
CME_ROUTER#show ephone

ephone-3[0] Mac: 1C39.470A.C906 TCP socket:[1] activeLine:0 whisperLine:0
REGISTERED in SCCP ver 9/9 max_streams=3
mediaActive:0 whisper_mediaActive:0 startMedia:0 offhook:0 ringing:0 reset:0
reset_sent:0 paging 0 debug:0 caps:7
IP:172.16.5.10 49580 CIPC  keepalive 4 max_line 8 available_line 8
Preferred Codec: g711ulaw

CME_ROUTER#configure terminal
CME_ROUTER(config)#ephone-dn 3
CME_ROUTER(config-ephone-dn)#number 1003
CME_ROUTER(config-ephone-dn)#exit
CME_ROUTER(config)#ephone 3
CME_ROUTER(config-ephone)#mac-address 1C39.470A.C906
CME_ROUTER(config-ephone)#button 1:3
CME_ROUTER(config-ephone)#restart
CME_ROUTER(config-ephone)#exit
CME_ROUTER(config)#exit
```

We can test this configuration by dialing the 1001 from ephone 3 and 1003 form ephone 1. Both calls should be successful.

❖ SIP

At this point we have one SCCP IP phone and one SCCP IP Communicator up and running. The SCCP IP phone has already downloaded firmware and we can continue with the SIP integration. To prevent problems with the SIP firmware download, we start with the SCCP firmware deregistration.

CME_ROUTER config (ch10c7):

```
CME_ROUTER#configure terminal

CME_ROUTER(config)#no tftp-server flash:apps42.9-2-1TH1-13.sbn
CME_ROUTER(config)#no tftp-server flash:cnu42.9-2-1TH1-13.sbn
CME_ROUTER(config)#no tftp-server flash:cvm42sccp.9-2-1TH1-13.sbn
CME_ROUTER(config)#no tftp-server flash:dsp42.9-2-1TH1-13.sbn
CME_ROUTER(config)#no tftp-server flash:jar42sccp.9-2-1TH1-13.sbn
CME_ROUTER(config)#no tftp-server flash:SCCP42.9-2-1S.loads
CME_ROUTER(config)#no tftp-server flash:term42.default.loads
CME_ROUTER(config)#no tftp-server flash:term62.default.loads
```

```
CME_ROUTER(config)#telephony-service
CME_ROUTER(config-telephony)#no load 7942
CME_ROUTER(config-telephony)#create cnf-files
Creating CNF files...

CME_ROUTER(config-telephony)#load 7942 SIP42.8-4-2S
CME_ROUTER(config-telephony)#create cnf-files
Creating CNF files...
CME_ROUTER(config-telephony)#exit
CME_ROUTER(config)#exit
```

We need to download and extract SIP firmware to the flash card of CME_ROUTER. The process is the same as for SCCP. Only file names are different. We can test the reachability of the PC1 just to be sure.

CME_ROUTER config (ch10c8):

```
CME_ROUTER#ping 172.16.5.10
Type escape sequence to abort.
Sending 5, 100-byte ICMP Echos to 172.16.5.10, timeout is 2 seconds:
.!!!!
Success rate is 100 percent (5/5), round-trip min/avg/max = 1/1/1 ms
```

We will use a CME_ROUTER to download files from a TFTP server that we already setup on PC1.

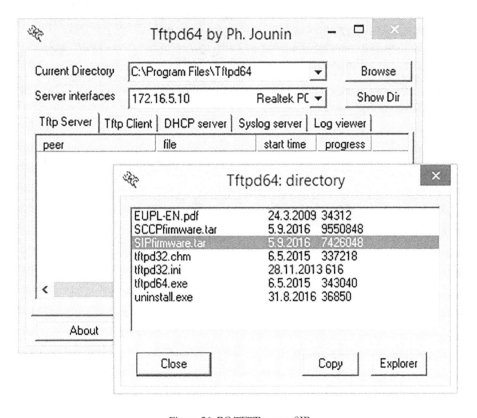

Figure 26: PC TFTP server SIP

In the next step, we download and extract SIP firmware files to the flash card of CME_ROUTER.

CME_ROUTER config (ch10c9):

```
CME_ROUTER#archive tar /xtract tftp://172.16.5.10/SIPfirmware.tar
flash:
Loading sip7942.tar from 172.16.5.10 (via FastEthernet0/0.50): !
extracting apps42.8-4-1-23.sbn (2918613 bytes)!!!!!!!!!!!!
extracting cnu42.8-4-1-23.sbn (485066 bytes)!!
extracting cvm42sip.8-4-1-23.sbn (3047459 bytes)O!!!!!!!!!!!!!
extracting dsp42.8-4-1-23.sbn (335003 bytes)O!
extracting jar42sip.8-4-1-23.sbn (630128 bytes)!!
extracting SIP42.8-4-2S.loads (656 bytes)O
extracting term42.default.loads (660 bytes)
extracting term62.default.loads (660 bytes)!
[OK - 7426048 bytes]
```

After a successful download and extraction all the files should be located on CME_ROUTER flash card. All the downloaded files have to be registered with the TFTP server (CME_ROUTER not PC1) to be reachable for the IP phone.

CME_ROUTER config (ch10c10):

```
CME_ROUTER#configure terminal
CME_ROUTER(config)#tftp-server flash:apps42.8-4-1-23.sbn
CME_ROUTER(config)#tftp-server flash:cnu42.8-4-1-23.sbn
CME_ROUTER(config)#tftp-server flash:cvm42sip.8-4-1-23.sbn
CME_ROUTER(config)#tftp-server flash:dsp42.8-4-1-23.sbn
CME_ROUTER(config)#tftp-server flash:jar42sip.8-4-1-23.sbn
CME_ROUTER(config)#tftp-server flash:SIP42.8-4-2S.loads
CME_ROUTER(config)#tftp-server flash:term42.default.loads
CME_ROUTER(config)#tftp-server flash:term62.default.loads
CME_ROUTER(config)#exit
```

We need to configure basic SIP CUCME parameters.

CME_ROUTER config (ch10c11):

```
CME_ROUTER#configure terminal
CME_ROUTER(config)#voice service voip
CME_ROUTER(conf-voi-serv)#allow-connections sip to sip
CME_ROUTER(conf-voi-serv)#sip
CME_ROUTER(conf-serv-sip)#registrar server expires max 1200 min
300
CME_ROUTER(conf-serv-sip)#exit
CME_ROUTER(conf-voi-serv)#exit
```

```
CME_ROUTER(config)#voice register global
CME_ROUTER(config-register-global)#mode cme

CME_ROUTER(config-register-global)#source-address 172.16.1.1 port
5060
CME_ROUTER(config-register-global)#max-dn 30
CME_ROUTER(config-register-global)#max-pool 10
CME_ROUTER(config-register-global)#load 7942 SIP42.8-4-2S
CME_ROUTER(config-register-global)#authenticate register
CME_ROUTER(config-register-global)#tftp-path flash:
CME_ROUTER(config-register-global)#create profile
CME_ROUTER(config-register-global)#exit
CME_ROUTER(config)#exit
```

Complete the following steps to perform factory reset of IP phone2 (other IP phone and IP Communicator leave unchanged). We use already mentioned procedure (123456789*0#). IP phone2 should download SIP firmware and register with the CUCME. All we need to do is to register SIP dn and assign it to the button on pool.

CME_ROUTER config (ch10c12):

```
CME_ROUTER#configure terminal
CME_ROUTER(config)#voice register dn 2
CME_ROUTER(config-register-dn)#number 1002
CME_ROUTER(config-register-dn)#exit

CME_ROUTER(config)#voice register pool 2
CME_ROUTER(config-register-pool)#id mac 10BD.0000.0002
CME_ROUTER(config-register-pool)#number 1 dn 2
CME_ROUTER(config-register-pool)#username 102 password 12345
CME_ROUTER(config-register-pool)#codec g711ulaw
CME_ROUTER(config-register-pool)#type 7942
CME_ROUTER(config-register-pool)#exit

CME_ROUTER(config)#voice register global
CME_ROUTER(config-register-global)#create profile
CME_ROUTER(config-register-global)#exit
```

The final step of this configuration task is a functionality test. We try to make calls between the IP Phones and the IP Communicator. We need to test all the possible combinations.

	SCCP IP Phone 1001	SCCP IP Communicator 1003	SIP IP Phone 1002
SCCP IP Phone 1001		OK	OK
SCCP IP Communicator 1003	OK		OK
SIP IP Phone 1002	OK	OK	

❖ Further study

It is advised to test the reverse hybrid scenario. Try to configure SIP as the first protocol followed by SCCP configuration. The order of partial configurations is important and perhaps a bit tricky. Try to experiment to achieve a functional solution.

❖ Quiz

1. SCCP and SIP protocols use the same firmware files?

    A. Yes
    B. No
    C. Only in 2016 CUCME version
    D. SIP only uses firmware files

    Answer: B

2. CUCME supports SCCP and SIP protocols

    A. Only one at the time
    B. Only SIP
    C. Only SCCP
    D. Both at once

    Answer: D

3. The call between SCCP and SIP IP phones

    A. requires special hardware connected to the CME_ROUTER.
    B. is not possible.
    C. is blocked by switch.
    D. is possible.

    Answer: D

4. How many MAC addresses IP Phone has with SCCP and SIP support?

    A. Only one
    B. None
    C. Five
    D. It has only IP address.

    Answer: A

5. Pool command is valid in

    A. Telephony-service
    B. Voice register
    C. Pattern
    D. SCCP
    E. Dn

    Answer: B

"Intentionally blank"

FINAL QUIZ

50 QUESTIONS

Complete the statements or choose the correct answer A, B, C or D. Only one option is correct if not stated otherwise.

1. Which address is borrowed from the DHCP server by an IP phone?

   A. Postal
   B. MAC
   C. IP
   D. SIP

2. The DHCP server can run on

   A. Cloud storage
   B. Router
   C. SIP
   D. SCCP

3. VLANs configuration is stored in

   A. vlan.dat
   B. vlan.conf
   C. flash.dat
   D. flash.txt

4. Rollover cable is designed for

   A. Console connection
   B. Overload protection
   C. Switch
   D. VTP

5. Select a routing protocol

   A. VTP
   B. RIP
   C. MAC
   D. SCCP

6. Which of the following is true regarding VTP?

   A. It only operates on a router.
   B. It is the only way to configure VLANs.
   C. A switch has assigned a client or a server role.
   D. It is useless on an IP network.

7. What is the purpose of the trunk between the switches?

   A. Transfer of multiple VLANs.
   B. Distribution of Option 150.
   C. Portfast functionality.
   D. DHCP pool.

8. What is PoE?

   A. A type of cable.
   B. Ping or Error.
   C. An advanced method of switch monitoring.
   D. Technology for distributing electrical power over the UTP.

9. How many IP addresses can be borrowed from the DHCP pool?

   A. None.
   B. With prefix /24 it is 255 addresses.
   C. It depends on configured pool size.
   D. Only 199 MAC addresses.

10. The hostname of the switch

   A. can be changed with the *hostname* command.
   B. is imprinted in hardware.
   C. is randomly generated on the boot.
   D. is a four digit number.

11. How do you assign the directory number 2004 to the first button on an IP phone?

  A. button 2004
  B. 2004 to 1 B
  C. button 1:2004
  D. flash 2004->1

12. Physical IP phone is represented in SCCP as

  A. an analog pool.
  B. XML Dn.
  C. an Ephone.
  D. a pool.

13. The file with the .TAR extension includes

  A. packed or archived files.
  B. tele-active response folders.
  C. the IOS.
  D. the TFTP address.

14. SCCP firmware

  A. is universal and it is stored in one file.
  B. depends on the IP phone type.
  C. is deleted after the IP phone downloads it.
  D. is the MAC dependent.

15. The TFTP server is required for

  A. the IP phone to be able to download firmware files.
  B. the time synchronization.
  C. the button deregistration.
  D. SCCP only.

16. *Preference* value equals to zero refers to

    A. the highest priority.
    B. the client role.
    C. the preference turned off.
    D. the null input.

17. Button separator "S"

    A. enables button overlay.
    B. disables the ring for any incoming calls.
    C. does not exist.
    D. enables the watch mode.

18. Is it possible to assign the ephone-dn automatically?

    A. No.
    B. Only dual-line.
    C. Yes, with the *auto assign* command.
    D. Yes, with the DHCP.

19. How many types of IP Phones are supported by the CUCME?

    A. 54.
    B. Default type.
    C. It is IOS specific.
    D. Five types in one network.

20. How many IP Phones can share the same template?

    A. Just two.
    B. Multiple.
    C. The template cannot be shared.
    D. 254 with SCCP.

21. Which codec is compatible with the Music on Hold feature?

    A. G798.
    B. mp3.
    C. G.711.
    D. SIP.

22. Which type of forwarding can be configured by the user?

    A. Dynamic.
    B. No-answer.
    C. Static.
    D. Intercom.

23. Which of the following represent transfer modes?
    (Select all that apply.)

    A. Immediate.
    B. On hold.
    C. Blind.
    D. Consult.

24. Which of the following is required for call parking?

    A. Additional ephone-dn.
    B. No additional requirements.
    C. The DHCP pool.
    D. The SCCP pool.

25. Which form of the paging generates less overhead on the network?

    A. Broadcast.
    B. Unicast.
    C. Multicast.
    D. Pagecast.

26. Which of the following allows us to connect an analog phone to the router?

    A. DNS.
    B. FBX.
    C. RJ45.
    D. FXS.

27. What is required to power the analog phone?

    A. PBX.
    B. Power brick.
    C. Electrical outlet.
    D. 230V.

28. Which firmware is required by an analog phone to function properly with CUCME?

    A. SIP and SCCP.
    B. No firmware is needed.
    C. SCCP only.
    D. Vendor's proprietary.

29. Which of the following are signaling methods associated with an analog phone? (Select all that apply.)

    A. DTMF.
    B. PSTN.
    C. PBX.
    D. PULSE.

30. Ringing frequency is specified in

    A. Farad.
    B. Newton.
    C. Hertz.
    D. Tesla.

31. Select VoIP proprietary protocol.

    A. SCCP.
    B. DHCP.
    C. SIP.
    D. RIP.

32. Is it necessary to replace the IP Phone during the migration from the SCCP to the SIP?

    A. Only in case of migration from the SIP to the SCCP.
    B. Only firmware has to be replaced.
    C. Change of topology is required.
    D. CUCME has to be reinstalled.

33. How can any IP phone acquire firmware from the router?

    A. TFTP.
    B. SCCP.
    C. VoIP.
    D. MAC.

34. Is it possible to calculate the MAC address from the IP address?

    A. Only 24 bits.
    B. Yes.
    C. No.
    D. Hexadecimal version only.

35. Which combination of the keys resets the IP Phone?

    A. 123#124#125#
    B. ##11##22##33
    C. *#987654321
    D. 123456789*0#

36. What represents the SIP pools in CUCME?

    A. DHCP addresses.
    B. Physical IP phones.
    C. Dial plan numbers.
    D. Buttons.

37. Is the SIP Shared line the mandatory part of all SIP calls?

    A. Only with SCCP.
    B. Inbound calls only.
    C. No.
    D. Yes.

38. The SIP Template

    A. is configured directly on the IP phone by the user.
    B. passes the configuration parameters to the multiple IP phones.
    C. is broadcasted by the router.
    D. is not supported by CUCME.

39. Is it possible to set the IP phone time value with the *time* command on CUCME?

    A. Only when it is down for maintenance.
    B. Only when there are no active calls.
    C. No.
    D. One IP phone at the time.

40. The SIP system message

    A. is not supported in *cme mode*.
    B. can only be 6 characters long.
    C. says "Your current call" by default.
    D. is omitted on SIP.

41. CUCME local directory

   A. is automatically created by CUCME.
   B. contains only manual entries.
   C. is already retired feature.
   D. is stored on the IP Phone.

42. Static call forwarding

   A. is the myth.
   B. can be overridden by dynamic call forwarding.
   C. is only supported by SCCP.
   D. is only supported by the specific device.

43. The SIP call transfer

   A. interconnects SIP and SCCP.
   B. requires functional softkey.
   C. is blocked by a switch.
   D. is the same feature as the Call pickup.

44. Dynamic SIP call forwarding

   A. is not supported by the pools.
   B. requires the park-slot.
   C. can be configured by the IP phone user.
   D. is blocked after three failed attempts.

45. Which command is suitable for blocking the SIP calls?

   A. black-list number
   B. exempt-number
   C. block-call
   D. after-hours

46. Is it possible for SCCP and SIP to coexist in the same CUCME?

    A. Yes.
    B. No.
    C. FXS is required.
    D. IP phones need united firmware.

47. The migration from SCCP to SIP

    A. is not possible without the flash card replacement.
    B. requires the firmware swap.
    C. is not possible without the new CUCME installation.
    D. is impossible.

48. The call between SCCP and SIP IP phones

    A. requires special hardware connected to the CME_ROUTER.
    B. is not possible.
    C. is blocked by a switch.
    D. is possible.

49. Is it possible to run SIP and SCCP simultaneously on a single IP phone?

    A. Only with the special SICP firmware.
    B. No.
    C. Yes.
    D. Only on the CISCO IP phones.

50. Is it possible to use the CISCO IP Communicator to make a call to a SIP IP phone?

    A. Telephony-service has to be disabled.
    B. It requires two pools to be assigned to the IP Communicator.
    C. Call transfer has to be active.
    D. Yes.

❖ Final Quiz Answer Sheet

	A	B	C	D
1.	A	B	C	D
2.	A	B	C	D
3.	A	B	C	D
4.	A	B	C	D
5.	A	B	C	D
6.	A	B	C	D
7.	A	B	C	D
8.	A	B	C	D
9.	A	B	C	D
10.	A	B	C	D
11.	A	B	C	D
12.	A	B	C	D
13.	A	B	C	D
14.	A	B	C	D
15.	A	B	C	D
16.	A	B	C	D
17.	A	B	C	D
18.	A	B	C	D
19.	A	B	C	D
20.	A	B	C	D
21.	A	B	C	D
22.	A	B	C	D
23.	A	B	C	D
24.	A	B	C	D
25.	A	B	C	D

26.	A	B	C	D
27.	A	B	C	D
28.	A	B	C	D
29.	A	B	C	D
30.	A	B	C	D
31.	A	B	C	D
32.	A	B	C	D
33.	A	B	C	D
34.	A	B	C	D
35.	A	B	C	D
36.	A	B	C	D
37.	A	B	C	D
38.	A	B	C	D
39.	A	B	C	D
40.	A	B	C	D
41.	A	B	C	D
42.	A	B	C	D
43.	A	B	C	D
44.	A	B	C	D
45.	A	B	C	D
46.	A	B	C	D
47.	A	B	C	D
48.	A	B	C	D
49.	A	B	C	D
50.	A	B	C	D

#	A	B	C	D		#	A	B	C	D
1.	A	B	**C**	D		26.	A	B	C	**D**
2.	A	**B**	C	D		27.	**A**	B	C	D
3.	**A**	B	C	D		28.	A	**B**	C	D
4.	**A**	B	C	D		29.	**A**	B	C	**D**
5.	A	**B**	C	D		30.	A	B	**C**	D
6.	A	B	**C**	D		31.	**A**	B	C	D
7.	**A**	B	C	D		32.	A	**B**	C	D
8.	A	B	C	**D**		33.	**A**	B	C	D
9.	A	B	**C**	D		34.	A	B	**C**	D
10.	**A**	B	C	D		35.	A	B	C	**D**
11.	A	B	**C**	D		36.	A	**B**	C	D
12.	A	B	**C**	D		37.	A	B	**C**	D
13.	**A**	B	C	D		38.	A	**B**	C	D
14.	A	**B**	C	D		39.	A	B	**C**	D
15.	**A**	B	C	D		40.	**A**	B	C	D
16.	**A**	B	C	D		41.	**A**	B	C	D
17.	A	**B**	C	D		42.	A	**B**	C	D
18.	A	B	**C**	D		43.	A	**B**	C	D
19.	A	B	**C**	D		44.	A	B	**C**	D
20.	A	**B**	C	D		45.	A	B	C	**D**
21.	A	B	**C**	D		46.	**A**	B	C	D
22.	**A**	B	C	D		47.	A	**B**	C	D
23.	A	B	C	**D**		48.	A	B	C	**D**
24.	**A**	B	C	D		49.	A	**B**	C	D
25.	A	B	**C**	D		50.	A	B	C	**D**

"Intentionally blank"

FIGURES

REGISTER OF ACRONYMS

AC	Alternating Current
CCNA	Cisco Certified Network Associate
CDP	Cisco Discovery Protocol
CLI	Command Line Interface
COM	Communication port
CUCME	Cisco Unified Communications Manager Express
DHCP	Dynamic Host Configuration Protocol
DNS	Domain Name System
DSP	Digital Signal Processor
DTMF	Dual-Tone Multi-Frequency
FXO	Foreign eXchange Office
FXS	Foreign eXchange Subscriber
GUI	Graphical User Interface
IEEE	Institute of Electrical and Electronic Engineers
IOS	Internetwork Operating System
IP	Internet Protocol
ISO	International Organization for Standardization
IT	Information Technologies
MAC	Media Access Control Address
NIC	Network Interface Card
OSI	Open System Interconnection
OUI	Organizationally Unique Identifier
PBX	Private Branch Exchange
PC	Personal Computer
PLAR	Private Line Automatic Ringdown
PoE	Power over Ethernet
PSTN	Public Switched Telephone Network
RIP	Routing Information Protocol
RJ12	Registered Jack 12
RJ45	Registered Jack 45
SCCP	Skinny Connection Control Protocol (also other definitions exist)
SIP	Session Initiation Protocol
SW	Switch
TCP	Transmission Control Protocol
TFTP	Trivial File Transfer Protocol
URL	Uniform Resource Locator
USB	Universal Serial Bus
UTP	Unshielded Twisted Pair
VLAN	Virtual Local Area Network
VLSM	Variable Length Subnet Mask
VoIP	Voice over Internet Protocol
XML	Extensible Markup Language

REGISTER OF CONFIGURATIONS

REFERENCES

[1]   Flanagan, W. (2012). The future of voice telephony and unifying
        communications. John Wiley & Sons Ltd.

[2]   Standards.ieee.org. (2018). Standard Group MAC Addresses: A Tutorial
        Guide. [online] Available at:
        http://standards.ieee.org/develop/regauth/tut/macgrp.pdf [Accessed 30 Jan.
        2018].

[3]   Droms, R. and Lemon, T. (2004). The DHCP handbook. Indianapolis,
        Ind.: Sams.

[4]   Odom, W. (2016). Cisco CCNA routing and switching ICND2 200-125.
        Cisco Press.

[5]   Cisco (2017). Unified Communications - Cisco Unified Communications
        Manager Express. [online] Cisco. Available at:
        https://www.cisco.com/c/en/us/support/unified-communications/unified-
        communications-manager-express/tsd-products-support-series-home.html
        [Accessed 30 Nov. 2017].

[6]   Cisco (2018). Understanding VLAN Trunk Protocol (VTP). [online]
        Cisco. Available at: https://www.cisco.com/c/en/us/support/docs/lan-
        switching/vtp/10558-21.html [Accessed 20 Oct. 2017].

[7]   Cisco (2017). Cisco IOS IP Configuration Guide, Release 12.2 -
        Configuring Routing Information Protocol [Cisco IOS Software Release
        12.2]. [online] Cisco. Available at:
        https://www.cisco.com/c/en/us/td/docs/ios/12_2/ip/configuration/guide/fip
        r_c/1cfrip.html [Accessed 20 May 2017].

[8]   Debian (2018). DHCP_Client - Debian Wiki. [online] Wiki.debian.org.
        Available at: https://wiki.debian.org/DHCP_Client [Accessed 31 Jan.
        2018].

[9]   Cisco (2017). Cisco Unified Communications Manager Express System
        Administrator Guide - System-Level Parameters [Cisco Unified
        Communications Manager Express]. [online] Cisco. Available at:
        https://www.cisco.com/c/en/us/td/docs/voice_ip_comm/cucme/admin/conf

iguration/manual/cmeadm/cmesystm.html#concept_hnt_nsp_nx [Accessed 31 Jan. 2018].

[10]   CallTower (2018). 7945, 7965, 7975 Factory Reset Procedure. [online] CallTower Solutions Center. Available at: https://www.uc.solutions/Cisco/002Phones/79XX_Series/7945%2C_7965%2C_7975_Factory_Reset_Procedure [Accessed 31 Jan. 2018].

[11]   Cisco (2018). Cisco Unified Communications Manager Express System Administrator Guide - Reset and Restart Cisco Unified IP Phones [Cisco Unified Communications Manager Express]. [online] Cisco. Available at: https://www.cisco.com/c/en/us/td/docs/voice_ip_comm/cucme/admin/conf iguration/manual/cmeadm/cmereset.html [Accessed 31 Jan. 2018].

[12]   Cioara, J. and Valentine, M. (2012). CCNA voice 640-461. Indianapolis, Ind.: Cisco.

[13]   Jounin, P. (2018). TFTP server. http://tftpd32.jounin.net: Philippe JOUNIN.

[14]   Cisco (2018). Upgrade IP Phone Firmware with CCME. [online] Cisco. Available at: https://www.cisco.com/c/en/us/support/docs/voice-unified-communications/unified-communications-manager-express/68244-PhoneLoadUpgradeCCME.html#configs [Accessed 31 Jan. 2018].

[15]   Cisco (2017). Cisco Unified Communications Manager Express Command Reference - Cisco Unified CME Commands: E [Cisco Unified Communications Manager Express]. [online] Cisco. Available at: https://www.cisco.com/c/en/us/td/docs/voice_ip_comm/cucme/command/r eference/cme_cr/cme_e1ht.html#wp2620327000 [Accessed 31 Jan. 2018].

[16]   Cisco (2018). Cisco IP Communicator. https://www.cisco.com/c/en/us/products/collaboration-endpoints/ip-communicator/index.html: Cisco.

[17]   Cisco (2018). Cisco Unified Communications Manager Express Command Reference. [online] Cisco. Available at: https://www.cisco.com/c/en/us/td/docs/voice_ip_comm/cucme/command/r eference/cme_cr/cme_e1ht.html#wp2620327005 [Accessed 8 Feb. 2018].

[18]   Cisco (2018). Cisco Unified Communications Manager Express Command Reference - Cisco Unified CME Commands: B [Cisco Unified

Communications Manager Express]. [online] Cisco. Available at: https://www.cisco.com/c/en/us/td/docs/voice_ip_comm/cucme/command/reference/cme_cr/cme_b1ht.html#wp2028848042 [Accessed 8 Feb. 2018].

[19] Cisco (2018). Cisco Unified Communications Manager Express System Administrator Guide - Configuring Phones to Make Basic Calls [Cisco Unified Communications Manager Express]. [online] Cisco. Available at: https://www.cisco.com/c/en/us/td/docs/voice_ip_comm/cucme/admin/configuration/manual/cmeadm/cmebasic.html#concept_61989333B94D45FBB13E6C69443C4CB4 [Accessed 8 Feb. 2018].

[20] Cisco (2018). Cisco Unified Communications Manager Express Command Reference - Cisco Unified CME Commands: A [Cisco Unified Communications Manager Express]. [online] Cisco. Available at: https://www.cisco.com/c/en/us/td/docs/voice_ip_comm/cucme/command/reference/cme_cr/cme_a1ht.html#wp2298232729 [Accessed 8 Feb. 2018].

[21] Cisco (2018). Cisco Unified Communications Manager Express Command Reference - Cisco Unified CME Commands: E [Cisco Unified Communications Manager Express]. [online] Cisco. Available at: https://www.cisco.com/c/en/us/td/docs/voice_ip_comm/cucme/command/reference/cme_cr/cme_e1ht.html#wp2316569335 [Accessed 8 Feb. 2018].

[22] Cisco (2018). Cisco Unified Communications Manager Express Command Reference - Cisco Unified CME Commands: T [Cisco Unified Communications Manager Express]. [online] Cisco. Available at: https://www.cisco.com/c/en/us/td/docs/voice_ip_comm/cucme/command/reference/cme_cr/cme_t1ht.html#wp1177319710 [Accessed 8 Feb. 2018].

[23] Cisco (2018). Cisco Unified Communications Manager Express System Administrator Guide - Modify Cisco Unified IP Phone Options [Cisco Unified Communications Manager Express]. [online] Cisco. Available at: https://www.cisco.com/c/en/us/td/docs/voice_ip_comm/cucme/admin/configuration/manual/cmeadm/cmelabel.html [Accessed 8 Feb. 2018].

[24] Cisco (2018). Corporate and Personal Directory Setup. [online] Cisco.com. Available at: https://www.cisco.com/c/en/us/td/docs/voice_ip_comm/cuipph/9971_9951_8961/10_0/english/adminguide/P567_BK_A27DADFD_00_adminguide-

8961-9951-9971-10_0/P567_BK_A27DADFD_00_adminguide-8961-9951-9971-10_0_chapter_01110.pdf [Accessed 9 Feb. 2018].

[25] Cisco (2018). Cisco Unified Communications Manager Express System Administrator Guide - Call Transfer and Forward [Cisco Unified Communications Manager Express]. [online] Cisco. Available at: https://www.cisco.com/c/en/us/td/docs/voice_ip_comm/cucme/admin/configuration/manual/cmeadm/cmetrans.html [Accessed 9 Feb. 2018].

[26] Cisco (2018). Cisco Unified Communications Manager Express System Administrator Guide - Call Park [Cisco Unified Communications Manager Express]. [online] Cisco. Available at: https://www.cisco.com/c/en/us/td/docs/voice_ip_comm/cucme/admin/configuration/manual/cmeadm/cmepark.html [Accessed 9 Feb. 2018].

[27] Cisco (2018). Cisco Unified Communications Manager Express System Administrator Guide - Intercom Lines [Cisco Unified Communications Manager Express]. [online] Cisco. Available at: https://www.cisco.com/c/en/us/td/docs/voice_ip_comm/cucme/admin/configuration/manual/cmeadm/cmeinter.html#wp1019638 [Accessed 9 Feb. 2018].

[28] Cisco (2018). Cisco Unified Communications Manager Express System Administrator Guide - Paging [Cisco Unified Communications Manager Express]. [online] Cisco. Available at: https://www.cisco.com/c/en/us/td/docs/voice_ip_comm/cucme/admin/configuration/manual/cmeadm/cmepage.html [Accessed 9 Feb. 2018].

[29] Cisco (2018). After-Hours Call blocking on CME. [online] Supportforums.cisco.com. Available at: https://supportforums.cisco.com/t5/collaboration-voice-and-video/after-hours-call-blocking-on-cme/ta-p/3118480 [Accessed 9 Feb. 2018].

[30] Cisco (2018). Cisco Unified Communications Manager Express System Administrator Guide - Music on Hold [Cisco Unified Communications Manager Express]. [online] Cisco. Available at: https://www.cisco.com/c/en/us/td/docs/voice_ip_comm/cucme/admin/configuration/manual/cmeadm/cmemoh.html [Accessed 9 Feb. 2018].

[31]   Cisco (2018). Configuring FXS Ports for Basic Calls. [online] Cisco.com. Available at: https://www.cisco.com/c/en/us/td/docs/ios/voice/fxs/configuration/guide/1 5_1/fxs_15_1_cg_book/fxsbasic.pdf [Accessed 9 Feb. 2018].

[32]   TelecomWorld 101 (2018). CME - Configuring the FXO port for a POTS line - TelecomWorld 101. [online] Telecomworld101.com. Available at: http://www.telecomworld101.com/CMEFXO.html [Accessed 9 Feb. 2018].

[33]   Cisco (2018). Cisco Unified Communications Manager Express: SIP Implementation Guide. [online] Cisco. Available at: https://www.cisco.com/c/en/us/support/docs/voice-unified-communications/unified-communications-manager-express/99946-cme-sip-guide.html [Accessed 9 Feb. 2018].

[34]   Cisco (2018). Cisco Unified Communications Manager Express Command Reference - Cisco Unified CME Commands: T [Cisco Unified Communications Manager Express]. [online] Cisco. Available at: https://www.cisco.com/c/en/us/td/docs/voice_ip_comm/cucme/command/r eference/cme_cr/cme_t1ht.html#wp2070969421 [Accessed 9 Feb. 2018].

[35]   Cisco (2018). Cisco Unified Communications Manager Express System Administrator Guide - Directory Services [Cisco Unified Communications Manager Express]. [online] Cisco. Available at: https://www.cisco.com/c/en/us/td/docs/voice_ip_comm/cucme/admin/conf iguration/manual/cmeadm/cmedirs.html [Accessed 9 Feb. 2018].

[36]   Cisco (2018). Cisco Unified Communications Manager Express System Administrator Guide - Call Blocking [Cisco Unified Communications Manager Express]. [online] Cisco. Available at: https://www.cisco.com/c/en/us/td/docs/voice_ip_comm/cucme/admin/conf iguration/manual/cmeadm/cmeblock.html#task_B03536651C894498A27F 467BFDBE70CD [Accessed 9 Feb. 2018].

Notes

Notes

rev.: 20200322

www.ingramcontent.com/pod-product-compliance
Lightning Source LLC
LaVergne TN
LVHW081342050326
832903LV00024B/1271